LIVING A RICHER LIFE

*Getting the Most out of Life's
Gifts and Circumstances*

Ervin (Earl) Cobb
Charlotte D. Grant-Cobb, PhD

Copyright © 2010 by Richer Life, LLC

Published and distributed by ‡RICHER Press
An Imprint of Richer Life, LLC

4600 E. Washington Street, Suite 300, Phoenix, Arizona 85034
www.richerlifellc.com

Cover Design: Richer Media USA

Photographs: Richer Media USA and iStock LP

No part of this publication may be reproduced, stored in a retrieval system, or transmitted in any form or by any means, electronic, mechanical, photocopying, recording, scanning, or otherwise, except as permitted under Section 107 or 108 of the 1976 United States Copyright Act, without prior written permission of the publisher.

RICHER Press books and products are available through most bookstores. RICHER Press also publishes its books in a variety of electronic formats. Some content that appears in print may not be available in electronic books.

Library of Congress Cataloging-in-Publications Data

Cobb, Ervin and Grant-Cobb, Charlotte D.
Living a Richer Life: Getting the Most out of Life's Gifts and Circumstances
1st edition
   p.   cm.
ISBN 978-0-9903291-3-8 (pbk : alk. Paper)
1. Self Help   2. Education   3. Psychology

ISBN 13: 978-0-9903291-3-8
ISBN 10: 0-9903291-3-8

Text set is Adobe Garamond
First edition, August 2010
Second edition, April 2012
Paperback, June 2013

Printed in the United States of America

DEDICATION

***

To our grandchildren
Jordan, Jayden and Destinee
May you have the opportunity to share our life's journey
with your children

***

In memory of our dear
Mother, Mrs. Carrie Bell (Washington) Cobb
who took her rightful place in heaven on June 29, 2009

In memory of our dear
Father, Mr. Artice Cobb, Sr.
who took his rightful place in heaven on February 16, 2013

***

In appreciation of Julius and Alberta Grant
Thanks to you both for your loving support

ACKNOWLEDGMENTS

Thanks to all of our family, extended family, adopted family and hundreds of teachers, professors, friends, co-workers and acquaintances who have been a necessary part of us. You have enriched our lives tremendously at strategic and critical times over the past half century. We will be forever grateful for your acceptance, friendship, encouragement, assistance, training, coaching, candor, support, advice, love and prayers.

Thanks to the wonderful colleagues and friends who, without hesitation, volunteered to collaboratively share their thoughts, insights and wisdom to improve this book. Special thanks to:

Ms. Yvette DeBois, M.D., M.P.H.
Aerospace Medicine

Mr. Robert J. Holmes, Ph.D.
Anthropologist and Linguist, Retired

Mr. Marvin Jackson, M.D.
Flight Surgeon, Federal Aviation Administration

Mr. Albert L. McHenry, Ph.D.
Professor Emeritus, Arizona State University

Mr. Lou Phillips
President and CEO, EthnoMediaGroup

Ms. Elizabeth Taylor, Ph.D.
Founder and President, Wisdom To Go™

CONTENTS

Preface xiii

Introduction xvii

Guide to Reading This Book xxiii

PART I: LIVING A RICHER LIFE

Chapter 1: Viewing Life as More Than a Collection of Events.............3

Chapter 2: Society Deprives Us of Self-awareness..................19

Chapter 3: Examining Your Life to Reveal Patterns of Behavior 29

Chapter 4: Behaviors that Can Add Richness to Your Life............35

Chapter 5: Special Gifts and Opportunities of Circumstance.........45

Chapter 6: Identify Opportunities and Live a Richer Life............53

PART II: A MODEL FOR LIVING A RICHER LIFE

Chapter 7: Using Models to Identify and Seize Opportunities 63

Chapter 8: Framing Mind-Set and Enhancing Perspective 71

Chapter 9: Who Am I Now? 83

Chapter 10: What Can I Learn? 89

Chapter 11: What Happened Along the Way? 95

Chapter 12: Why Does Quality and Alignment Matter?..................101

Chapter 13: When is Re-invention Par for the Course? 107

Chapter 14: Why Does it Come Back Ten-fold?..........................113

Chapter 15: A Model for Living a Richer Life...............................119

PART III: OPPORTUNITIES REVEALED: PERSONAL NARRATIVES

Chapter 16: "A New House for Mom and Dad"........................ 131

Chapter 17: "Staying in Our Daughter's Life"............................141

Chapter 18: "Becoming a Franchise Owner"..............................153

Chapter 19: "Joining the Betterliving™ Family".........................165

PART IV: NAVIGATING THE LIFE ENRICHMENT MODEL™

The Life Enrichment Model™ *Application Guide*......................185

The Life Enrichment Model™ *Reference Sheets*........................195

The Life Enrichment Model™ *Glossary of Terms* 223

About the Authors 231

Select Bibliography...233

PREFACE

"Circumstances are the rulers of the weak; they are but the instruments of the wise." - **Samuel Lover**

Whether you like it or not, major events in life happen and then come the circumstances.

Getting a good grasp of the role that *events* and *circumstances* play in your life is essential to you understanding how to shape more positive outcomes to challenging situations. Achieving this level of consciousness is also essential to you recognizing and valuing the difference between *responding* versus simply *reacting* to a circumstance.

For various reasons, many of us have not thought a lot about the difference between a life event and a life circumstance. Prior to writing, *Living a Richer Life* we had not given it much thought either.

However, through our research for the book and close reflection upon a number of major events and circumstances from our past — we discovered that for many years we had actually used an inherent process that recognized and valued such a distinction. It became apparent that by doing so, we benefitted greatly from how we internalized the events and how we responded to the surrounding circumstances.

Let's start by answering the question, "What distinguishes a life event from a life circumstance?" Then, we will discuss why recognizing and valuing this distinction can make a significant difference in how you view the circumstance and your ability to shape a more positive outcome.

Most events in life are fairly common. Most result in minor changes in your life and in your lifestyle. However, there are events that can cause significant turmoil and change in your life. Among them, we would include:

- A marriage;
- The birth of a child;
- A major salary increase;
- Becoming the caretaker of an aging parent;
- The purchase of a new home;
- A felony DWI conviction;
- The death of a spouse;
- A long-term loss of employment;
- A permanent disability;
- A chronic illness;
- An early retirement;
- A home foreclosure;
- Personal bankruptcy;
- A teenage pregnancy; and
- Winning of the lottery.

Some of these events are planned. Some even fall into the category of life accomplishments. Others, unfortunately, are the result of being in the wrong place at the wrong time. While others appear to be curve balls thrown at you and can suddenly seem unfair, unclear and certainly unexpected.

Now, circumstances, on the other hand, are conditions or facts that determine [or must be considered in determining] a course of action. Circumstances, in most cases, are the result of a single event or a sequence of events that can change our daily existence. What was once so easily in our grasp, such as a promising career, a beautiful home or a loving friend, can disappear in an instant. However, it is also true that circumstances can serve as powerful catalysts. They can assist you in enacting and realizing significant changes in your life.

Many people unconsciously forfeit their ability to understand and control the outcomes caused by major events that unexpectedly surface in their lives. They do this, all too often, by reacting versus responding to the circumstances surrounding the event. Some of them act as if it's an inevitable conclusion that they will suffer a periled consequence, lose something that is special to them or feel a certain way based on a particular set of circumstances.

However, did you know that in almost every case it is not the actual event itself that causes life's most challenging ups and downs? The cause of the most helpful and the most harmful life changes you experience as a consequence of a major life event is how you internalize what the event means to you and your response to the circumstances that accompany the event.

For example, a teenage pregnancy is accompanied by circumstances which could involve addressing the need to complete a good education and to find the wherewithal not to allow an early life event to derail career and lifelong aspirations. The winning of a cash lottery can become *unrewarding* unless timely investment, relationship and privacy management steps are taken to address circumstances which may cause a *bigger purse* to turn into an even *bigger headache*. With your proactive and well-planned response, the outcome to each of these events [an unexpected pregnancy and winning the lottery] could enrich your life and the lives of people around you. Without such a response, dreams could be lost and relationships could be ruined for a lifetime.

When you more thoughtfully respond versus simply react to circumstances which surface as a result of an event, you can more effectively shape a desired outcome. You can also minimize negative impacts that life's inevitable events may have on the quality of your life and the lives of people you love.

Armed with a clear understanding of the significance of the event, a well-crafted response and the control of your humanistic gifts, you can seize potential opportunities which are embedded within life's inevitable circumstances.

Even though the concept of *reacting* versus *responding* to major circumstances may appear naturally obvious, it is not as easy as it seems. Most people instinctively "react" to surprises and unexpected changes in their life.

As we all get older, we become conditioned by customs and our daily environment. This conditioning, in many cases, allows predetermined reactions to replace more mindful responses. In addition, many of us tend to not recognize the institutional influences which are at odds with our ability to gain broader perspectives of important situations and respond in a manner which shapes the most positive outcomes.

In Chapter 1 of this book, you will find a discussion of a paradigm we constructed to assist you in your understanding of the various environmental and human behavioral factors that come into play when you encounter major circumstances in your life. The paradigm is called the *Life Enrichment Continuum*™. We suggest that you spend some time reviewing the "Enrichment Principles" and "Enrichment Challenges" set forth in the Life Enrichment Continuum™. Integrating concepts similar to those presented in this paradigm into your thought process can help you recognize influences which may be preventing you from more effectively responding to major circumstances in your life.

By doing so, you will significantly increase the number of positive outcomes in your life, minimize the number of negative outcomes and live a richer and more abundant life.

INTRODUCTION

"People seldom improve when they have no other model but themselves to copy after." - **Oliver Goldsmith**

"When a society is rich and triumphant, its people start to ask not just what can be had from life but how can I live a life that's worth living," says Martin Seligman, former president of the American Psychological Association. The demand for products and programs that will allow Americans to improve their relationships and business skills, make more money, lose weight, cope with stress or obtain a quick dose of motivation continues to increase. Now, more than ever, Americans are turning to gurus for help in a variety of areas. According to the psychological geniuses, Americans want to be more in control of their emotional and financial lives.

Well, we are neither gurus nor psychological geniuses. We are just two hard working Americans who grew up in working class families. We, like millions of working class Americans, were fortunate enough to raise a healthy family, work our way through college and work hard enough to carve out rewarding careers. We were also fortunate enough to build a network of friends and business acquaintances that have been instrumental in providing emotional and spiritual support.

However, we both have had a life-long interest in improving ourselves, our lives and the lives of those around us. Over the years, we have not viewed our personal or professional improvement activities as laborious tasks.

To the contrary, we have framed these activities as "journeys" or "passages" that illuminate our paths and crossroads as we move from one stage or phase of life to another.

It was almost exactly ten years ago when we started to first reflect on the many gifts we had received and the unavoidable circumstances we had encountered during our thirty years together. We were winding down a corporate position with the Reynolds and Reynolds Company and we had just moved from Dayton, Ohio to a lovely area just north of Charlotte, North Carolina called Lake Norman. We fondly recall a series of long nights spent sitting on the sun porch overlooking the calming movements of the massive lake.

For hours on end, we discussed the events, difficult decisions, rewarding accomplishments and heartbreaking disappointments we had encountered over three decades of building professional careers, supporting community activities and assisting family members while raising our own. It was during these colloquies when we began to feel the necessity to take a new journey. This journey would lead us to chronicle and to examine gifts and circumstances that most significantly contributed to or diminished the richness---*quality, fullness and abundance* --- in our lives.

When we started this journey we were quite secure in our spiritual beliefs and the grace of God. Thus, we were not looking for answers as to "why" events in our lives had unfolded as they had --- good or bad. Through our Christian experience, we both have always known who is in ultimate control. Our goal here was to enlighten ourselves by examining the earthly factors involved in how we navigated through many of our life's challenges and opportunities. We had no indication, at the time, that our work would result in the writing of "Living a Richer Life."

Nonetheless, we were acutely aware from our own day-to-day experiences that "societal dimensions or factors" [i.e. family-birth privileges, educational level, decision-making skills and relationships] along with how we innately respond to them, must have played a significant role in determining the outcomes we had experienced. The only questions in our minds were:

Which factors have the most influence and when? How much control, on a daily basis, do we have on affecting our behavior and life's outcomes? What governs our responses to our greatest challenges and circumstances? and Whether or not the "lessons we would learn" could be effectively shared with others?

As fate would have it, we thoroughly enjoyed our latest journey and were quite pleased and somewhat surprised with what it revealed. In satisfying our curiosity regarding the influence of societal factors on life's outcomes, we gained fresh insight regarding ourselves, our relationships and how our priorities in life had indeed influenced many significant outcomes. Moreover, our research and analysis also revealed a unique view of a repeatable "pattern of events" or process associated with directly and indirectly influencing positive versus negative outcomes.

It was the surprising discovery of this contemporary approach or "model" which initially ignited our excitement around the writing of this book. The practicality by which this interactive, deductive model combines self-examination and a sincere consciousness of the influence that societal and behavioral factors have on life's outcomes is truly insightful. Through repetitive and random evaluations, it is apparent that the model, when properly applied, is uniquely capable of consistently revealing opportunities for life enrichment.

Our purpose for writing *Living a Richer Life* is two-fold.

First, we want to share with you how we have been able to live an amazingly richer and abundant life by consistently minimizing the negative impact of potentially life altering events. As we learned from our journey, we were able to shape positive outcomes to many of our most difficult events by effectively *responding* versus *reacting* to the surrounding circumstances. Based on the revelations and insights we gained from our intense reflection upon and analysis of our responses, we unearthed and are now able to share the collection of concepts, perspectives and practices which made this possible. The essence of which is embodied in what is now known as the *Life Enrichment Continuum*™. This novel and contemporary paradigm is the product of over ten years of study, research and collaboration. All of which were constructed to serve as an original process to aid in examining and chronicling the significant events in our lives together over the past thirty years.

Secondly, we want to offer you the opportunity to walk with us "down the path" of appreciating the concepts and assumptions set forward in the paradigm. The goal is for you to learn how to utilize the *Life Enrichment Model*™ to improve your ability to effectively respond to life altering circumstances. When properly applied, the *Life Enrichment Model*™ can become an exceptional tool to aid in identifying unforeseen opportunities and determining the paths available to you which have the potential of leading to a more satisfying and prosperous life.

We have written this book in a conversational fashion. We intentionally repeat many of the fundamental concepts and characterizations in several locations throughout the book. Our goal is to personally corroborate your understanding of the *Life Enrichment Continuum*™ paradigm and the deductive model's composition so that you can effectively use your individual *powers of revelation* to connect the various components based on where you are along the *Continuum of Life*.

We have organized this book in four distinct parts.

Part I, *"Living a Richer Life"*, establishes the foundation for the thesis of how you can live a richer life by identifying enrichment opportunities which are embedded in many of the circumstances you encounter during your lifetime. This part of the book discloses how the revelations surrounding a contemporary view of living in today's America were transformed into an extremely useful paradigm for life enrichment. This novel paradigm is now called the *Life Enrichment Continuum*™.

Chapter 1 concludes with a detailed summary of the *Life Enrichment Continuum*™ and reveals the paradigm's *Enrichment Principles* and corresponding *Enrichment Challenges*. Chapters 2 through 5 investigate how self-awareness, human behavioral patterns and a methodical approach to recognizing and identifying life's gifts, circumstances and opportunities are all instrumental to a contemporary life enrichment process. Chapter 6 introduces innovative approaches to identifying opportunities for life enrichment. In addition, it outlines the school of thought we used to develop a *Two-Step Opportunity Recognition Methodology*. This methodology aids in identifying the most favorable "starting point" for entering the Opportunity Examination process.

In Part II, *"A Model for Living a Richer Life"*, we walk you through what was required of us, during our journey, to accurately recall, analyze and examine the events and circumstances documented in our life chronicle. This part of the book outlines the underlying schools of thought as well as the assumptions and guidelines that were constructed in order to deductively examine potentially life altering circumstances and reveal life enrichment opportunities. These assumptions and guidelines, along with uniquely designed queries [required to properly *frame* our state of mind at the time of the life event] ultimately formed the basis of what evolved into what is now known as the *Life Enrichment Model*™.

In Chapter 7, we give further details about the objective of our journey to chronicle most of the memorable events and circumstances we had encountered over the past thirty years. We also share with you the steps taken to recall and document how we approached and examined the circumstances that surrounded each major event. This chapter concludes with a discussion of how we were somewhat forced to unearth a method to more expediently examine circumstances, retrospectively, to address the accumulating volume of chronicle entries. This discussion reveals how our diligent search for this methodology led to the utilization of deductive modeling techniques. In addition, we share with you a summary of our research surrounding the idea of using *models* and *deductive reasoning* to explore and reveal tradeoffs, uncertainties, options and sensitivities surrounding human actions.

The remainder of Part II introduces the school of thought underlying some of the most valuable components of the *Life*

Enrichment Model™, called *Framing Elements*. Here, we also discuss the *Framing Element's* role in the Enrichment Opportunity Examination process. Chapter 8 addresses the school of thought behind why *Framing Elements* are considered so important to the life enrichment process and the measure of life in the 21st century. Chapters 9 through 14 present a depiction of each of the six *Framing Elements* and the reasoning behind the modeling components' ability to approximate our "mind-set" as ascertained through our level of "self-awareness" at the time we encounter a life altering circumstance. Part II concludes in Chapter 15 with a detailed overview of all of the components of the *Life Enrichment Model*™ as well as a narrative and illustrative presentation of the *Life Enrichment Examination Process*.

Part III, *"Opportunities Revealed: Personal Narratives"*, presents a sample from our collection of narratives which chronicle and examine significant events that have occurred in our lives over the past thirty years. The four narratives presented in Chapters 16 through 19 are original and unaltered. It is our hope that our candor will provide you some meaningful insight into how we used the concepts personified in the *Life Enrichment Model*™ to help us approach the challenges and circumstances we encountered.

Part IV, *"Navigating the Life Enrichment Model*™*"*, includes an Application Guide to aid you in navigating and applying the model to situations that you may be encountering now or in the future. Also included are Reference Sheets which support the modeling process and a Glossary of Terms.

We hope you enjoy your life's journey as much we are enjoying ours.

Guide to Reading This Book

A Note from the Authors

During our extensive collaboration with friends and colleagues regarding various aspects of this book, we were asked on several occasions, *"Who should read this book ... and how?"*

Recognizing that we had purposefully packed *Living a Richer Life* with an ample supply of intriguing *thoughts, topics and tools* which could easily be *explored, expanded and exercised* for a lifetime, we were somewhat compelled to include this note.

Of course, we believe that anyone who could benefit from a fresh and innovative approach to significantly enhancing their ability to effectively *respond* versus *react* to major circumstances in their life should read this book *cover-to-cover* and immediately take advantage of the innovative guidance provided by the *Life Enrichment Model*™.

As all of us travel along the Continuum of Life, our *self-improvement* and *life management* requirements will vary depending on our stage in life and *what life tosses our way*.

Obtaining the maximum benefit from certain concepts, exercises and tools within this book may also vary based on your *stage of life*. However, as you will acquire from this book, *maximizing positive outcomes* and *minimizing negative outcomes* to potentially life altering circumstances at *all* stages are critical to *living your best life --- from your teenage years, through middle age and beyond retirement.*

We recommend the following as a general guide to potential categories of readers as well as what might be considered the most *relevant topics*, by category, to be explored more deeply.

- **Teenagers and Young Adults** – *Patterns of Behavior, Enrichment Elements, Archetypes and Lessons Learned from the Personal Narratives.*

- **Young Professionals and Young Couples** – All of the above, plus the *Life Enrichment Continuum™, Societal Influences, Use of Special Gifts and Opportunities of Circumstance.*

- **Seasoned Professionals and Mature Couples** – All of the above, plus *the application of the Life Enrichment Model™ and its methodologies to all major events and circumstances in your life.*

- **Self-Improvement Seekers** -Particularly those interested in more effectively addressing *"earthly circumstances"* in order to *live the very best life* that their "Maker" has planned for them…cover-to-cover and enjoy!

We wish you the best in your life's journey.

PART I

LIVING A RICHER LIFE

"There is no right or wrong way of living this wondrous journey, but if we can live it the best possible way we can, enjoying everything around us, being in "this moment", constantly growing and learning, appreciating and loving, we would be much richer for it." **- Unknown**

CHAPTER ONE

VIEWING LIFE AS MORE THAN A COLLECTION OF EVENTS

"Life is not a continuum of pleasant choices, but of inevitable problems that call for strength, determination, and hard work." - **Indian Proverb quote**

"It's not true that life is one damn thing after another; it is one damn thing over and over." - **Edna St. Vincent Millay**

As you may have gained from the introduction, our lives individually and as a couple have been filled with gratifying *ups* and painful *downs*. The process of documenting our life's reflections has revealed many gifts and circumstances associated with overcoming personal and professional challenges. It has also revealed how we achieved many of our life's goals and yet were gravely disappointed, on some occasions, with people and situations that robbed our lives of potentially richer moments.

However, the most intriguing revelation uncovered during the examination of our life's challenges, opportunities and choices was that

--- the more we examined our lives, the more we thought about where we've been, how we got there and where we're going.

The more we examined, the happier we became in anticipating our future. We are sure you've read this quote before: "*The unexamined life is not worth living.*" It is accredited to Socrates and his soliloquy to his accusers during his trial for heresy. Socrates was being charged with encouraging his students to challenge the accepted beliefs of the day. Facing a sentence of death, Socrates had the option of choosing a different punishment. He could have chosen life in prison or life in exile and he would likely have avoided the death sentence.

Socrates believed that the only thing that made life useful was to be able to examine the world around him and discuss how to make [himself and thus] the world a better place. He strongly believed that without his "examined life" there was no point in living.

Fortunately, none of us must choose between an examined life and death. But the sad thing is that most people avoid leading an examined life. However, avoiding examining your life, in our thesis, forfeits the opportunity to live a more *satisfying and richer* life.

It was at the dawn of the 21st century, December 1999, when the idea of creating a chronicle and reflecting on how we approached the circumstances surrounding major events in our lives over the past thirty years first surfaced.

We had just completed a second move of residency in less than three years. We left the beautiful sunsets and upscale lifestyle of Scottsdale, Arizona and moved to the diverse cultural richness of the mid-west. Then, we moved to the southern charm and freshness of the new South.

We were still celebrating some other important changes and additions in our life. They included the completion of a new retirement home we built for our Georgia parents, the achievement of the family's first doctorate degree, the purchase of a national retail franchise and a very good corporate severance package [following the sale of the Healthcare Systems business which brought us to the Midwest] which paved the way for a smooth transition to a new lake home in North Carolina.

As we had done for decades, we considered these kinds of events in our life as personal blessings and gifts that we attempted to never take for granted. We were also beginning to view ourselves, for the first time, more as entrepreneurs versus the corporate employees that we had been for the last twenty-five years.

So, our need to reflect upon and examine our life did not come during a period when we were down and out. It was actually just the opposite. Neither of us could recall what exactly triggered this scholarly and emotional drive to create this chronicle and to become more aware of our past decisions, choices and behaviors. We still wonder why we felt so passionate about the idea. We vividly recall the desire to dig deeper into the research and how the "chronicle idea", as we initially called it, became a priority for both of us at the time.

Maybe somewhat like Socrates, we were at the stage in our lives where we felt a need to understand more about the world around us and how to make [us and] it better. In a conversation during the 1999 Christmas holidays, we agreed that the one thing we were both sure about was that if we did began this journey, we needed to establish and document *a comprehensible view or perspective* of life --- as it relates to dealing with life's many circumstances. In other words, a perspective or vision which characterizes the factors involved as we all encounter and respond to daily circumstances as average Americans in the 21st century.

Chapter 1 of this book sets the stage for recalling the many discussions, intensive research and creative assessments which intellectually and socially engaged us during our ten year journey. The goal is to establish the foundation for the thesis this book sets forth: *We all can live a richer life by getting the most out of life's gifts and circumstances.*

In this chapter we also disclose, for the first time, how our revelations surrounding a contemporary view of living in today's America transformed into an extremely useful paradigm for life enrichment. This paradigm is now called the *Life Enrichment Continuum*™.

While creating our chronicle and examining how we managed events in our life over a substantial period of time, the paradigm's assumptions, concepts, practices and beliefs became an important anchor. We used the paradigm to reconstruct the *mind-set* we needed to gain invaluable and coherently insightful analysis of our responses to past circumstances, the actions that were taken and, retrospectively, the nature [good or bad] of the outcomes.

The *Life Enrichment Continuum*™ provided us a systematic approach to characterizing [in a practical manner] the various environmental and human behavioral factors that come into play when any of us encounter circumstances in life.

It did not take a significant amount of research for us to determine that most Americans desire and aspire to being in the position to positively navigate the outcomes resulting from encounters with daily circumstances.

Yet, it has been substantiated that most of us feel that we seldom find ourselves in this position. Our research and the insights gained from developing the *Life Enrichment Continuum*™, as an aid to assist in examining our own life experiences, have convinced us that the ability to live a richer life *truly lies within each of us*. It only requires that each of us take the time to understand what is involved in this somewhat complicated process. We also are required to learn how to effectively and consistently integrate the guidance of life enrichment principles into our daily lives.

You will note throughout this book, that the enrichment principles set forth by the *Life Enrichment Continuum*™ are essential to establishing the *mind-set* required to perform a holistic and knowledgeable examination of life circumstances. The *Enrichment Challenges*, as presented later in this chapter, provide a valid starting point for the assembly of thoughtful and targeted responses to shape positive, life enriching outcomes. This paradigm embodies the school of thought which led us to surmise the following as the premise of our belief that getting the most out of life's gifts and circumstances can lead to living a richer life.

Our premise can be surmised as follows:

We all desire and aspire to be in the position to positively navigate the outcome of our encounters with daily circumstances. However, there are some circumstances that we face in life that challenge our normal abilities to quickly respond in a manner that prevents significant setbacks. These types of circumstances may have the potential of not only impeding the addition of richness in our lives but may actually rob us of many of the human and physical assets we have already obtained.

In these cases, we must first take the time to understand how such a circumstance can be transformed into a life enriching opportunity. Then, we must proactively approach the situation with purpose, knowledge and an acute awareness of our individual gifts [natural and acquired], in order to shape long lasting, positive outcomes.

The remainder of Chapter 1 presents a straightforward summary of the *Life Enrichment Continuum*™.

In Chapters 2 through 6, we share with you the thoughts and research which construct the case that a wholehearted sense of self-awareness, a fundamental understanding of behavioral patterns and a caring approach to recognizing and identifying life's gifts, circumstances and opportunities are instrumental to contemporary life enrichment. We also outline the reasoning as to why the ability to transform major challenges into life enrichment opportunities is within everyone's reach.

A Comprehensible Perspective of Life

Before we started on our journey to examine our gifts and circumstances we decided that we needed a framework which provided a comprehensible view or perspective of life in America as it relates to encountering life's circumstances.

We envisioned this *comprehensible perspective* taking the form of a set of ideas, conditions and assumptions which characterize the factors involved in shaping our thoughts, emotions, beliefs, and decision making as we encounter and respond to daily circumstances. The goal was to create a systematic approach to characterizing, in a practical manner, the various situational, environmental and behavioral dimensions that come into play when any of us encounter major circumstances in life.

We first drafted several lists of attributes that we believed would be involved in this type of characterization. The final version of the list included:

1. Time;
2. Circumstances;
3. Human gifts and qualities;
4. Opportunities for enrichment and enhanced quality of life;
5. Negative outcomes;
6. Positive outcomes;
7. A measure of life's richness; and
8. External and internal influences which affect an individual's perception and human behavior.

When we analyzed the list of significant events and circumstances created as a part of our life chronicle, there emerged a distinct correlation between the type of life event and our initial perception of the circumstances surrounding it. We also noticed that the chronological age bracket that we were in at the time of the occurrence seemed to affect the thought process we used to arrive at responses.

Our observations revealed that our most significant and emotional challenges occurred when we were in our twenties and thirties. This was during the time when we were busy building professional careers, raising our family and establishing a presence in our community. The events we encountered during our forties and fifties appeared to involve close relationships, such as our daughter finding herself, losing close friends and caring for aging parents.

The most significant challenges encountered at any point over this time span all left us drained. Some left us picking up broken pieces; while others resulted in memories of cherished additions to our life's richness. The additions or gifts we recalled receiving over this period included earning multiple college degrees and six figure incomes; purchasing great houses to call home; enjoying a wonderful marriage, a beautiful daughter and precious grandchildren; cultivating loving friendships and taking advantage of the opportunities to enjoy our parents as adults.

It also became obvious to us during this deep reflection that, on a consistent basis, the outcomes we perceived as negative seemed to always impede positive events we expected to occur during various stages of life i.e. periodic career moves, increases in income and the growth of certain valued relationships. While outcomes we perceived as positive appeared to somewhat significantly enhance our measure of richness --- such as happier family reunions, the house on the lake and the perfect place to worship.

As a result, it became even more evident to us that there were *predictable* and *all-pervading* dynamics common to encountering undeniable life circumstances. Our observations substantiated that the dynamics were present regardless of the specific nature of the event.

We summarized our observations as follows:

- *The somewhat predicable dynamics or patterns at hand as we encountered life circumstances seemed to differ in dimension, magnitude and structure as we traveled from one stage of our life to the next. However, their occurrence and influence on our perception and response mechanisms were not necessarily balanced in terms of the magnitude of the event and the time of the occurrence.*

- *There seemed to be an ubiquitous connection or correlation between how we perceived the predictability of outcomes regarding certain types of circumstances and where we found ourselves in terms of personal growth [mental, educational, intellectual, financial and spiritual] and our perceived social status at the time.*

- *There also seemed to be a relationship between our perception of the level of richness in our lives [at a given point in time over the past thirty years] and the quality of personal and professional relationships. Involved in this perception was how we viewed our relationships with others who had direct or indirect influence on our quality of life i.e. our family members, our friends, our boss, our co-workers, our pastor, our attorney, our doctors, our teachers, our daycare workers and etc.*

In search of a practical approach to creating this comprehensible perspective of life we spent several months discussing the possibilities with many of our friends, colleagues and acquaintances. We combined passionate debates and our observations with intensive research of published literature on related topics, such as human qualities, societal influences on group think and the fundamentals of human behavior.

We were particularly interested in how average Americans, like ourselves, approached the circumstances they encountered during their lifetime. We were also curious about how positive vs. negative outcomes affected the level of richness in their lives over time.

After much consternation, we finally arrived at a set of ideas, concepts and assumptions we now call the *Life Enrichment Continuum*™ --- a paradigm which characterizes the factors involved as we encounter and respond to daily circumstances in life.

We used the essence of this paradigm during the examination of the events we had chosen to include in our life chronicle. During this long and meticulous task we relented to mapping a process or model which would allow us to more efficiently and consistently arrive at the characterization of each action we had taken and the outcomes we had experienced.

The remainder of this chapter presents a summary of the *Life Enrichment Continuum*™ paradigm. This section is purposefully constructed to provide a progressive and illustrative portrayal as well as a comprehensive description of the concepts set forward within the paradigm.

Part II of this book examines and outlines the components of the deductive process or model we originally created to identify and examine life enrichment opportunities associated with the events documented in our chronicle.

The Life Enrichment Continuum™

The *Life Enrichment Continuum*™ paradigm provides a systematic approach to characterizing, in a practical manner, the various environmental and human behavioral influences that come into play when any of us encounter circumstances in life.

The *Life Enrichment Continuum*™ is summarized in this section in terms of its four basic *Enrichment Principles* and corresponding *Enrichment Challenges*. Each Enrichment Principle sets forth a thought provoking observation regarding the environment and the forces at play when you find yourself in the position in life where you must encounter a potentially life altering circumstance. Integrating the Enrichment Principles into your *"theater of thought"* during these times assists in establishing the *state of mind* optimum to properly identifying embedded enrichment opportunities.

The corresponding Enrichment Challenges constitute the knowledge-based objective or target we should all attempt to achieve as each of us shape our responses to the circumstances which surround major events. Collectively, the Principles and Challenges establish the framework required to move us into position to get the most out of life's gifts and circumstances.

I. **ENRICHMENT PRINCIPLE No. 1 - As we travel along the continuum of life, from one stage to the next, we accumulate insights and experiences which alter how we perceive** ourselves, how we perceive others and how we respond to opportunities for life enrichment.

As we all mature in life, our attitudes, values, knowledge, beliefs and behavioral patterns change over time. This process is a natural phenomenon in life and evolves through a series of physical, emotional and intellectual life stages. The most common stages are associated with our chronological evolution, such as teens, twenties, thirties, forties etc. We may actually display characteristics in several stages simultaneously, but our behavior patterns will likely be centered in a single stage.

As illustrated in Figure 1-1, as we all age and move along the *Continuum of Life*, we are presented with opportunities for life enrichment. However, we frequently do not readily recognize many of the opportunities, which are embedded within the circumstances we encounter. Many of us have looked back on events and circumstances in our lives and have said to ourselves or others, "If I only had known then, what I know now".

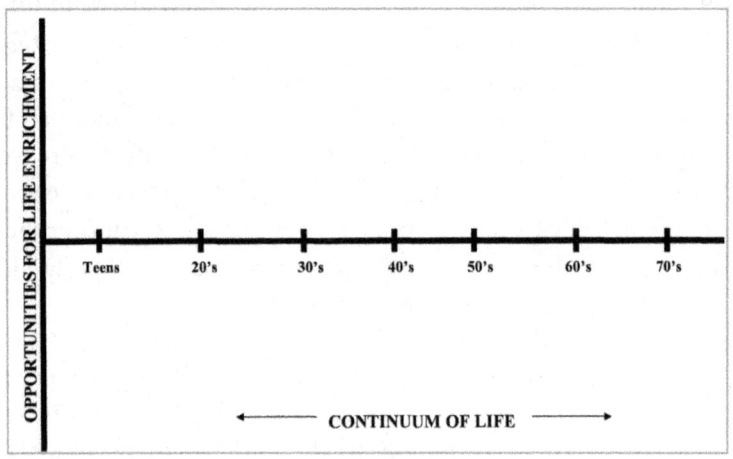

Figure 1-1 - Life Enrichment Continuum™

Many of the same challenges you encounter in your twenties and thirties are viewed quite differently when you are in your forties and fifties. Therefore, circumstances which may have caused significant turbulence in your lives during an earlier stage may result in significantly different outcomes at a point when you are further down the *continuum of life*. Your ability to recognize when circumstances can be used as life enrichment opportunities as well as the skills to leverage your gifts and shape positive outcomes increase with the experience, maturity and wisdom you accumulate as you travel along the *continuum of life*.

At any point in time along the *continuum of life*, you are the *same person* (i.e. in terms of DNA) and yet you are *different*. You accumulate life experiences essential to life enrichment as you acquire varying levels of self-awareness, education, relationships and decision making skills. Also, in the later stages of life you may reach a level of self-actualization which leads you to begin to think about reaching your full potential and shaping your legacy.

ENRICHMENT CHALLENGE No. 1 - *To recognize life enrichment opportunities presented to us as we travel along the Continuum of Life and to leverage the experience, maturity and wisdom we have accumulated by shaping our behaviors, perceptions and responses in order to take advantage of these opportunities.*

II. **ENRICHMENT PRINCIPLE No. 2 - Negative outcomes as a result of encountering a circumstance, at any time along the *continuum of life*, can and most often impede life enrichment. Positive outcomes have both near and long term impacts and, in most cases, significantly enhance the richness [i.e. quality, fullness and abundance] in our lives.**

As noted previously, as all of us travel along the *Continuum of Life* we inevitably will encounter challenges and circumstances. As we will be discuss in Chapter 4, the responses and behaviors to the stimulus associated with challenges and circumstances are heavily influenced by our humanistic qualities and our *Perceptual Filters*. Perceptual filters are categorized as *Sensory Screens* [seeing, hearing, feeling, smelling and tasting], *Emotional Screens* [personality, self-concept, attitudes, beliefs and habits], *Learning* and *Motivation*.

Your behavior in response to an event is a major factor in determining the event's *outcome* i.e. the conclusion, impact, affect and result. Your encounters with life's challenges and circumstances will inevitably generate outcomes that will impact your future.

Positive outcomes tend to significantly enhance the level of richness in your life and have both near-term and long-term impacts. *Negative outcomes* seem to always be accompanied with setbacks and have the potential of impeding growth and prosperity.

As shown in Figure 1-2, negative outcomes to challenges and circumstances *impede* life enrichment. Positive outcomes to the same challenges and circumstances can enhance richness and prosperity.

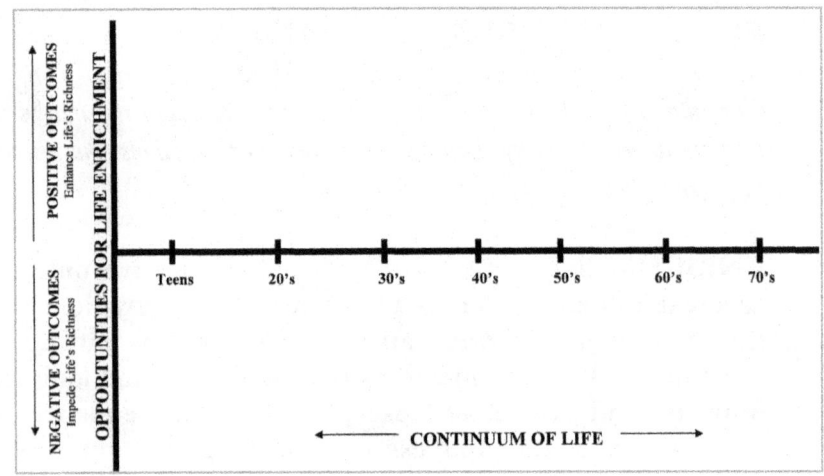

Figure 1-2 - Life Enrichment Continuum™

ENRICHMENT CHALLENGE No. 2 - *To leverage the refinement and growth of our humanistic gifts (qualities) as we travel along the Continuum of Life in order to facilitate as many positive outcomes and eliminate as many negative outcomes as possible.*

III. ENRICHMENT PRINCIPLE No. 3 – The measure of richness in our life is based on the societal norms of the day and is an omnipresent perception which significantly

influences our behaviors and responses to life's challenges and circumstances.

As we all progress along the *Continuum of Life*, the influences of society (i.e. culture, social order and humanity) becomes greater and plays an important role in shaping how we perceive ourselves, others and the circumstances we encounter along the way.

As illustrated in Figure 1-3, when your *measure of richness* dips below *typical*, it launches the perception [in your mind and the minds of others] of possessing a level of richness which is *below societal norms*; while measures above typical create the perception of possessing *above normal levels* of richness.

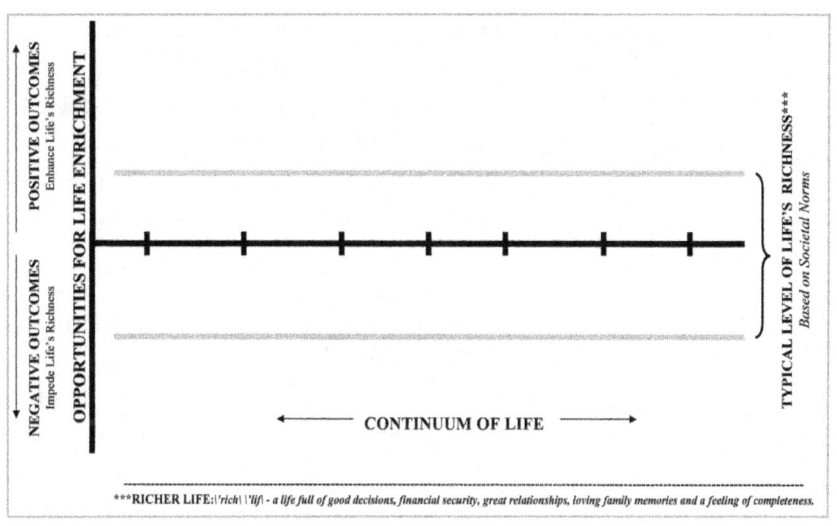

Figure 1-3 - Life Enrichment Continuum™

ENRICHMENT CHALLENGE No. 3 - *To maintain an awareness and perspective of the norms that are in vogue within society and to establish our own individual measure and perception of richness in our life as we respond to life's challenges and circumstances.*

IV. ENRICHMENT PRINCIPLE No. 4 – Positive outcomes which result from taking advantage of enrichment opportunities later in life may have the potential of

significantly offsetting the impact of negative outcomes experienced during earlier stages in our life.

As illustrated in Figure 1-4, we all are constantly encountering challenges and circumstances throughout our lifetime. Most encounters are characterized as *typical events*. Some result in positive outcomes and others in negative outcomes. However, events characterized as typical are all within what society views as normal, day-to-day life events.

The diagram also shows that some encounters may take the form of *life altering events*. Life altering events may include a high school and/or college graduation, a loving marriage, the birth of a child, a major promotion on the job, the opportunity to travel abroad or the winning of a state lottery --- in these cases, the events are all seen as having the opportunity to *enhance* the level of richness in our lives.

There may also be other life altering events which appear to have the opportunity to *impede* life enrichment. These may include dropping out of school, an unplanned pregnancy, being laid-off or fired from a job, a debilitating injury, a nasty divorce or a sudden death of a family member.

However, it is possible for the long term positive outcome to any one of the events in the examples above to potentially be either impeding or enhancing based on how each of us are able [and are in position] to emotionally, intellectually, physically or financially respond at the time it occurs. This thought is consistent with the axiom: *It is not necessarily the change, but how we respond to the change.*

Another school of thought in this observation and also illustrated in Figure 1-5 is that life altering events with positive outcomes may significantly offset events with negative outcomes. This "offsetting", over time, serves to turn a life perceived as less than typical [due to negative outcomes early in life] into one which possesses an above typical level of richness due to positive outcomes later in life. This thought is consistent with the axiom: *It's not how we start the race but how we finish.*

ENRICHMENT CHALLENGE No. 4 - *To enrich our lives to the fullest, we must not only recognize enrichment opportunities embedded within life altering circumstances but we must also take the actions necessary to ensure that we fully realize [gain the full impact of] as many positive outcomes as possible.*

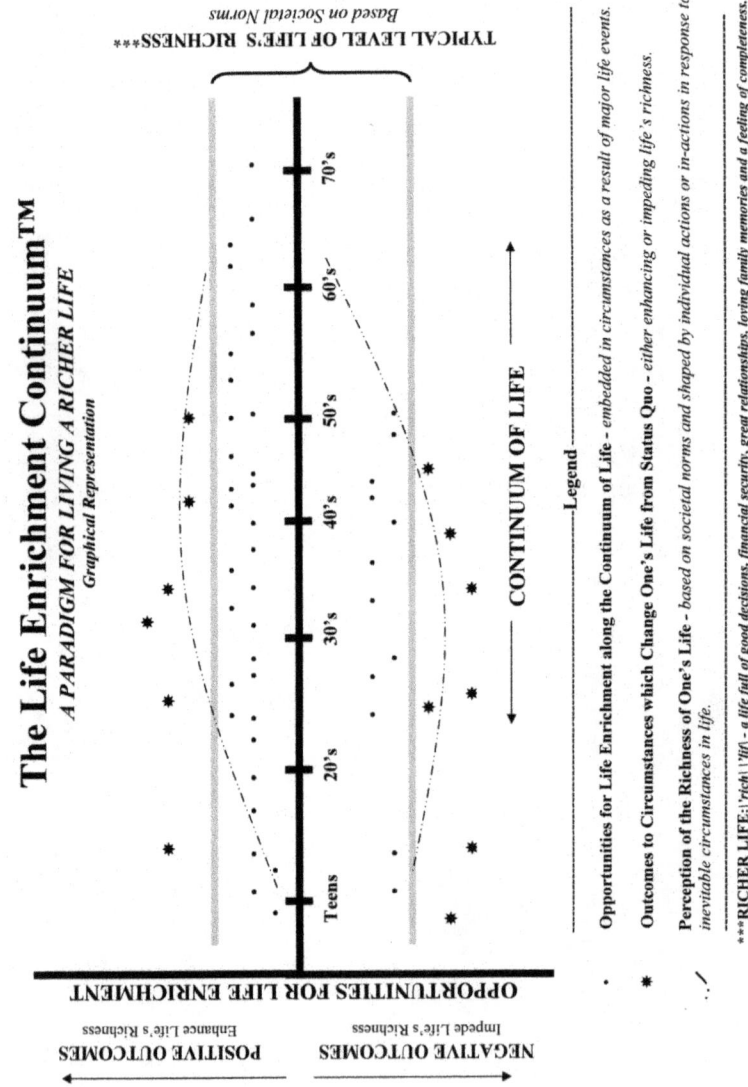

Figure 1-4 - Life Enrichment Continuum™

CHAPTER TWO

SOCIETY DEPRIVES US OF SELF-AWARENESS

"Most of the change we think we see in life is due to truths being in and out of favor." - **Robert Frost**

As we concluded our short stay in Dayton, Ohio in November 1999 and moved to a new home in the Sterling Point neighborhood of Lake Norman, North Carolina, we found ourselves with a precious opportunity. After twenty-five years of climbing the corporate ladder, we finally had some quality time to reflect on various aspects of our life's entire journey.

During this period, as we enjoyed the somewhat pleasant southern winter, we began to have more frequent discussions with each other regarding our life adventures and the life we have lived together. As a result of many conversations and invaluable dialogues with friends and associates, it quickly became apparent that the task of finding the time needed to examine our lives seemed the equivalent of defying gravity. In other words, it seemed that today's society was designed to pull the average American in so many other directions and somewhat discourage self-awareness.

Another challenge we discovered was that even though there have been hundreds of books written on the topic of self-awareness, many Americans do not have a good sense of what it really means to be self-aware. In our search to gain a practical understanding of self-awareness, we found several classical definitions. They included: awareness of your own individuality; a literal consciousness of one's self; the state or property of being self-aware; the ability to know and understand one's self; and a conscious knowledge of one's own character, feelings, motives and desires.

We have always thought of self-awareness as a way for us to explore our individual personalities, value systems, beliefs, natural inclinations, and tendencies. Because you are different in the way you react to things, how you learn and the methods by which you synthesize information, it's helpful to occasionally spend time in self-reflection to gain a better insight into yourself.

The following is a list of common areas where you may differ and thus may perceive and respond to similar situations in different ways.

- Preferred learning styles
- Aptitude for specific career fields
- Natural academic ability (mathematics, English, etc.)
- Personality traits (introvert, extrovert, sensitive, judgmental, etc.)
- Religious beliefs
- Political viewpoints
- Values (ethical, with integrity, scrupulous, etc.).

In our research, we found that self-awareness plays a major role in getting us through the day. When you have a better understanding of yourself [who you are], you are empowered to make changes and to build on your areas of strength.

You are also better positioned to identify areas where you need to make improvements not only within yourself but also in the environment in which you live and the people you have in your life. Self-awareness is often a first step to goal setting and factors significantly in your ability to reach them. It is also a major component which contributes to *framing* and shaping the state of mind required for you to live a more abundant and richer life.

Our research revealed three areas which appeared to us to be the most dominate factors in discouraging the average American from seriously engaging in a thorough self-awareness exercise.

The factors we identified can best be described as follows:

- A diminishing level of emotional honesty as we mature in life;

- The cycle of working and consuming that keeps us too busy to slow down for self-reflection; and

- The fact that, in many ways, society teaches us to ignore, repress, deny and lie about our feelings.

In the remaining sections of this chapter we present a detailed description of each of these factors. In addition, we include our thoughts on why we consider these factors to be so dominating in discouraging self-exploration. The last section of this chapter includes some suggestions on how we all may be able to create the environment, on a daily basis, required to bring more clarity, joy and richness into our lives.

A Diminishing Level of Emotional Honesty

It was not until we moved back to Arizona in 2006 and had the opportunity to live near our young grandchildren that we were able to confirm a belief that we both have had for a long time. That is, *"we all arrive on earth fully equipped"* with what make us *who we really are* [personality, wherewithal and spirit].

When our daughter, who will turn 33 this year, was growing up, we both were fully engaged in high profile corporate careers. Fortunately, there were extended family around us and we were successful in managing our travel schedules such that neither of us was required to be out of town at the same time. However, with our own daughter, we did not easily recognize the moments within her early childhood development which confirmed this belief [of arriving on earth fully equipped].

On the other hand, while watching our second grandson, on almost a weekly basis, transition from a delightful 10-month old infant to an even more delightful 5-year old, it was clearly obvious that we do arrive fully equipped --- including a generous portion of emotional honesty. Based on his personality, natural gifts and honest reactions to life's circumstances at a very early age, we could easily envision how our grandson would respond to life circumstances at age 14 and at age 44. This assumes that all of his gifts will be allowed to blossom and mature along with his age. It now appears that the capability to more readily recognize this phenomenon i.e. *"we all arrive on earth fully equipped"* is one of the major differences between *parenthood* and *grand-parenthood*.

Even at a young age we all tend to know which emotions we are feeling and why. You realize the links between your feelings and what you think, what you do and what you say. You recognize how your feelings affect who you really are, as well as your natural responses to the circumstances you encounter in life. Thus, you are born with a guiding awareness of what you later get to know as life's values, goals and richness.

To be emotionally honest, you must first be emotionally aware. This emotional awareness is related to what is called emotional intelligence. It is your emotional intelligence, combined with the necessary learning, practice and experience which give you the ability to accurately identify your feelings.

Emotional intelligence may also give you the ability to decide when it is in your best interest to be emotionally honest by sharing your genuine feelings. There are times when it is not healthy or safe for you to be emotionally honest. However, research reveals that, in general, you would be better off individually and as would society if you would be more emotionally honest --- particularly when you encounter life altering circumstances.

If you are more emotionally honest with yourself, you will get to know your "true self" on a deeper level. This could help us become more self-accepting. It also could help you make better choices about how to spend your time and who to spend it with.

If you are emotionally honest with others, it may encourage them to be more emotionally honest with you. When you are emotionally honest, you are more likely not to be asked or pressured to do things which you do not want to do. You will also find out sooner who respects your feelings.

Research in this area consistently reveals that emotional honesty is instrumental in achieving an elevated degree of self-awareness. Unfortunately, as we all mature in concert with life's stress and strain, our level of emotional honesty tends to diminish as we travel along the *Continuum of Life*. However, time is not the only major aspect associated with the lack of emotional honesty. Another key factor is how you naturally react to societal inferences and how your behavioral patterns reflect other's expectations.

As you develop close relationships with others and interact with groups within society, you tend to influence the moods of others. Influencing another person's emotional state, for better or for worse, is perfectly natural. We all do it constantly. Some say we "catch" emotions from each other similar to catching a social virus. This emotional exchange appears to amount to an invisible interpersonal economy in America and other societies. It is a part of every human interaction, but it is usually too subtle for us notice.

Expanding our Emotional Intelligence

Fortunately, according to experts, emotional intelligence and honesty at the levels required to build an elevated level of self-awareness can also be learned and developed.

Our research indicates that, individually, we are all capable of expanding our skill sets and increasing our level of emotional intelligence as we move through the various stages of our lives. The first step in developing emotional honesty with others is to become more self-aware of your own emotions.

One suggestion of how to become more aware of your emotions at different times in your life is to maintain a personal journal describing your feelings regarding specific situations and circumstances. By writing your feelings down, you may be able to better identify and become aware of your specific feelings during certain situations or at certain times. Figure 2-1 presents an example of such a journal or *emotional inventory*. As you become more aware of your daily emotional experiences, you can increase or expand your natural levels of emotional intelligence.

Depressed	Forgetful	Proud
Lonely	Stupid	Guilty
Happy	Angry	Afraid
Excited	Jealous	Connected
Bored	Inferior	Competent
Wanted	Incompetent	Powerless
Frustrated	Content	Overjoyed
Overwhelmed	Under-whelmed	Open-minded

Figure 2-1 - Emotional Inventory

When self-awareness is more fully developed within your own emotional experience you can then began the progression of sharing these emotions with others and moving forward in the practice of discovering opportunities to enrich your life in the future.

During our journey to chronicle and examine the significant events in our life, we spent days on end attempting to gauge our emotional honesty at various points in time over a thirty year period. For each of the events and circumstances we chronicled and examined, we devised a method to factor into our examination the role *emotional honesty* and *behavioral influences* played in the decision making process at various stages of our life. As our research has concluded, these and other humanistic qualities contributed to how we responded to the events and circumstances we encountered.

The Cycle of Working and Consuming

It did not take much research for us to be convinced that, as Americans living in the fast-paced, technology driven 21st century, most of us have cycles of working and consuming that keeps us too busy to slow down for self-reflection.

Most of us have worked 40 or more hours a week since we were 18 years old and will do that until we are well into our sixties or seventies. A recent report revealed that one in four American workers work more than 49 hours a week. One in eight Americans work more than 60 hours a week and one in ten hold down more than one job. As Americans, we have added 20 extra work days to our work year since 1970. It has been noted that American factory workers work an average of five weeks a year in overtime alone. We also work two months more per year than the French and the Germans. The questions that come to mind are: *Why do we do it? Do we need the money? Do we know how to live any other way?*

Some say that it's consumer-capitalism's game plan that prefers an unaware and vaguely dissatisfied populace that tries to fill the emptiness inside with shiny new products. We, as Americans, make up only 5% of the world's population, but we consume more than 25% of the world's resources and energy.

Regardless of the reasons, our society discourages self-awareness with an almost religious cycle of working and consuming that keeps all of us too busy to slow down for self-reflection. In our research we wanted to identify ways that we could integrate into our work and family life that would restore some harmony, reduce stress and allow us to find more work-life balance.

Here are six of the best suggestions we could find.

1. Don't lose sight of priorities.

Envision your own funeral. What is it that you would like for people to say about you and your legacy? If the people who eulogize you only comment on your stock portfolio, the number of degrees you have earned, the kind of car you drove and the size of your home --- they would say that those were your priorities.

If their comments were that you were an excellent father, mother, sister, brother, uncle, aunt or friend --- they would say that those were your priorities. With all the competition for our time and attention, it is easy to forget what is most important.

2. Take something off your to-do list.

Are there things on your list that could be removed without major consequences? Is every trip to the mall, every meeting or gathering in the community, every party or social event or every phone conversation really necessary? Are your expectations about your home chores unrealistic? Are your tasks focused on your priorities? Sometimes skipping something and seeing if it is missed is a good strategy.

3. Don't be afraid to use the word "No."

Is your presence critical at every meeting or social event to which you are invited, or could a few comments before or after the event suffice? Can you remind your boss, your client or your friend of what you are working on or doing when you are asked to do something new? Can you train your subordinates [as well as spouse, kids and relatives] not to "delegate upward" when bringing problems or concerns to you? Be cautious of those things to which you say yes, because it increases the other things to which you must say no.

4. Make good use of downtime.

Those of us who have a significant commute to work can choose to make the commute productive or relaxing, or can simply give in to road rage and frustration. How you use this valuable time is your choice. When we were working in the Washington DC area and commuting home to North Carolina every other week via U.S. Airways, we had a "to read" file in our briefcases. We took advantage of the opportunity of a few minutes of free time to do something meaningful. It is important to look for these kinds of opportunities.

5. Schedule time for yourself.

Who says that blocks of time on your calendar have to involve a meeting with or doing something for others? Schedule a meeting with yourself and keep the appointment. Block out time for working on a tough project. Schedule and take uninterruptible time for personal or professional development. Say yes to your health.

6. Sleep in a Storm.

We came across this tale in Mitch Albom's true story "Have a Little Faith". It presents a state of preparedness and control of our lives that we all should aspire to include in our life management portfolio.

> *"A man seeks employment on a farm. He hands his letter of recommendation to his new employer. It reads simply, 'He sleeps in a storm'.*
>
> *The owner is desperate for help, so he hires the man.*
>
> *Several weeks pass, and suddenly, in the middle of the night, a powerful storm rips through the valley.*
>
> *Awakened by the swirling rain and howling wind, the owner leaps out of bed. He calls for his new hired hand, but the man is sleeping soundly.*
>
> *So, he dashes off to the barn. He sees, to his amazement, that the animals are secure with plenty of feed.*
>
> *He runs out to the field. He sees the bales of wheat have been bound and are wrapped in tarpaulins.*
>
> *He races to the silo. The doors are latched, and the grain is dry.*
>
> *And then he understands. 'He sleeps in a storm'."*
>
> --- Mitch Albom's true story *"Have a Little Faith"*

Society and Our Feelings

We learned early in our life together that feelings are the body's way of communicating with you. If any of us ignore our feelings there is a high probability that things get worse, instead of better.

All of our feelings and emotions directly influence our actions and reactions. However, we do not want them to dominate us. Today's society often sees emotions as a sign of weakness. Thus, we have become accustomed to setting our feelings aside to be perceived more rational. Most of us will always have to deal with feelings no matter how logical and rational we appear.

Your emotions permit you to communicate with your *humanness* like no other sense of being. If you listen to society and try to uncouple yourself from your feelings, you may place yourself in more peril than if you simply live by your own feelings. The latter may give you a roller coaster approach to life. But, to pay no attention to your feelings may be devastating to the desire to enrich your life based on your needs. Many of us portray the result of not following our own feelings as potentially devastating because our feelings are like our nerve endings. Your feelings permit you to enjoy life to the fullest as well as warn you of peril.

In addition, your feelings serve as an important "check and balance" system. They steer you toward what is right and away from what is wrong. Closing your eyes to your emotional *check and balance* could permit you to do things that are harmful to yourself and to others.

You will never enjoy life to its fullness by avoiding your feelings. You have been given these magnificent feelings to aid in realizing your purpose in life. Using all of your senses to live *is* richer living. There is enormous value in striving to live a balanced and high quality life style.

We were fortunate to learn a long time ago that living a richer life is indeed, dependent on our total well-being.

CHAPTER THREE

EXAMINING YOUR LIFE TO REVEAL PATTERNS OF BEHAVIOR

"He who does not remember the past is condemned to repeat it."
- **Santayana**

Our research in the area of behavioral responses reveals that in the daily lives of most Americans, each day is filled with conscious and unconscious patterns of behavior.

These behaviors generally evolve around all our day to day experiences and the "societal dimensions or factors" which influence them. Deeper examination yields an understanding of the subconscious programming that essentially runs our lives. Surprisingly, we also discovered that unless we become aware of these patterns, much of our life is unconscious repetition.

While researching human patterns of behavior, we found that most of us only began to manage and control the patterns in our lives when we take the time to consciously reflect back over our lives. Unfortunately, in too many cases, this retrospective review only occurs during or after a significant emotional event such as a hardship, a divorce or a death in the family.

When we examined the events and circumstances we encountered in our early life together as a part of our chronicle development, we began to recognize distinctive behavior patterns in our relationships with family and friends, our co-workers, our daughter and generally throughout many aspects of our life. They were *behaviors* which had become normal activities we performed on a day-to-day basis such as calling each other sweetheart when greeting each other, calling home when one of us would be working late and reserving Saturday mornings to take bike rides with our daughter when she was younger.

However, it was difficult for us, even during examination, to distinguish the repeating processes while they were a part of our normal day-to-day activities. In general, it is difficult for any of us to see these "patterns" in daily life until after we have been through the event several times and perform some type of retrospective review.

Most of us generally do not understand why patterns in our life happen. The repetition of some patterns may cycle within weeks. Yet, others take months or years. The recurrence of some patterns may require a change in jobs, neighborhoods, churches, friends or relationships before the action occurs again. But, research in this area indicates that without a doubt, upon close observation, these distinctive patterns will reveal themselves.

As we further researched this topic, the questions that surfaced in our minds and deserved a deeper understanding were: *Why are patterns in our life important? Why do we need to learn to recognize patterns in other's lives? and How can we recognize the cycle of patterns required to live a richer life?*

Because each of us live differently in many ways, your patterns will certainly not be identical with patterns of others. This does not suggest that patterns are necessarily good or bad. However, the recognition of patterns and seeking to understand the underlying reasons for their existence helps all of us to become more conscious of why we behave the way we do and why we take certain actions.

Why are Patterns in our Life Important?

We discovered that patterns are characteristically a normal development. To some degree all of us construct patterns in order to make our lives more predictable, more controllable and less stressful. For example, each of us has a morning routine that helps us wake up in the morning, say hello to the world and get to work on time. We recall how for years, when we were climbing the corporate ladder, we both had very distinct patterns in our nine to five lives. One of us would get up at 4:00 AM in the morning, go for a two mile run, return home, take a shower and off to work. The other had a similar routine which included either an exercise class at the local gym or a brief work-out in the den of our home. Families with children have routines that help create security and consistency around the house and when they are apart. It appears that all patterns trend toward serving each of us in some fashion.

In our research of various types of patterns, we learned that some patterns reduce stress from traumatic events or difficult situations which may take physical and/or emotional tolls. Some patterns are unhealthy and can sometimes become destructive, i.e. smoking or drinking too much alcohol.

However, when you ask a smoker about why they smoke, they most often suggest that it's for relaxation. Some patterns are simple habits or routine practices. Yet, some patterns present themselves and prove to be long term solutions to a problem. In all cases, patterns are an important part of living. Most of us use patterns to answer questions, produce outcomes, organize confusing experiences or minimize stressful situations in our lives.

Why it's Important to Recognize our Life Patterns

Research indicates that most patterns are not necessarily alarming or worrisome. Patterns work to assist you in your daily efforts to organize your life, function at peak levels of performance and achieve life goals. It appears that the most critical time to recognize and evaluate the intrinsic value of patterns in your life is when you are responding to circumstances in your life. It is also helpful to recognize patterns when things are happening around you that you do not understand.

The following types of questions are characteristic of alarming patterns or patterns that repeat without you feeling that you are in control:

- Why am I on my 3rd job in two years?
- Why are my children not taking advantage of the life style they are privileged to have?
- Why have I not reached the level of career success that I feel I have earned?
- Why does my family appear to be pulling further apart vs. coming closer together?
- Why is the school system not providing the quality of education that my kids deserve?
- Why can't I stay in a relationship?
- Why do the relationships I cultivate always turn out the same?
- Why do I have such a hard time managing my money?

It is important to recognize these disconcerting patterns in your life so that you can adequately address them.

Why Do We Need to Learn to Recognize Patterns in Others Lives?

According to experts, sometimes the people that many of us care about most need our help. It appears that they do not seem to recognize and cannot stop the same self-defeating behaviors that have been impeding their ability to live a richer and more abundant life. Usually as an outsider, you can see the patterns that are occurring.

However, it still appears to be mysterious to many of us as to why someone we are close too and love continues to behave in a certain manner. Several examples may include: your children who cannot succeed in school despite good intelligence and hard work; a dear friend who does not have the drive to go beyond a dead-end job, but never seems happy; and a successful acquaintance and colleague who drinks excessively for no apparent reason.

It seems that we learn to recognize patterns in other's lives because we all would like to be of assistance to those we care about. We would do almost anything to see them become free of harmful behaviors or self-damaging activities. You may find it easier to recognize the patterns in others than in yourself. However, the question still looms as to how you can recognize the cycle of patterns in your own life.

How Can We Recognize the Cycle of Patterns that are Essential to Living a Richer Life?

Through further research, we discovered that when it comes to conversations regarding changing behavior, most of us do not respond well to vague or unclear messages. Our reactions to messages from within or from others that are vague or unclear may include frustration, anger, helplessness, pain or avoidance.

These behaviors produce an awakening defense against these feelings. The methods by which we all choose to defend ourselves may produce detrimental behavior. According to experts on the subject, detrimental behaviors are consistently used as a way to reduce the stress that can form disconcerting patterns of interaction. They also may result in poor coping skills that could eventually result in repeated negative outcomes in our lives.

When you decide to change disconcerting patterns, a trusted method, guide or model to lead you through a well-defined process of change can be extremely helpful. Why a model? Unfortunately, the disconcerting patterns are best understood by most of us when we are in a position to compare them to a set of more positive behaviors. We all tend to feel safer living with the "patterns we know" regardless of how destructive they may be. Research also indicates that an easy to understand model can provide the constructive direction required for recognizing and changing the patterns in our lives.

Based on the experience we have gained during our journey, we believe that constructive models can aid in assisting all of us in recognizing disconcerting behavioral patterns. Models that capture our attention and provide focus can also contribute to enhancing self-awareness and choosing paths that lead to living a richer life.

CHAPTER FOUR

BEHAVIORS THAT CAN ADD RICHNESS TO YOUR LIFE

"Behavior is a mirror in which every one displays his own image."
- Johann Wolfgang von Goethe

"All forms of self-defeating behavior are unseen and unconscious, which is why their existence is denied."- **Vernon Howard**

Prior to our examination of the challenges and circumstances we had encountered in our life, we extensively researched the nature of human behaviors in general.

We both were acutely aware from our own day to day experiences that "societal dimensions or factors" must have played a significant role in determining the outcomes we had experienced. We consider such factors to include family birth privileges, educational opportunities, decision making skills and personal & professional relationships.

Our research in this area led us to more clearly understand one of the most significant components involved in determining how we innately respond to societal factors is our behavioral system. Consequently, we were compelled to further examine the classes of behaviors that we found as most prevalent among the average American who describes him or herself as living a richer and more abundant life.

From our perspective a *richer life* is a life full of good decisions, financial security, great relationships, loving family memories and a feeling of completeness. It was our belief that if we map, *situation-by-situation* and *circumstance-by-circumstance*, the obvious with the not-so-obvious i.e. *why, when, whom and how* we could gain more visibility into what it takes to move down the paths associated with living a richer life based on 21st century measures.

The idea of constructing a map or record which characterizes the events over a thirty year period provided the momentum for our journey.

However, it was the early research of human behaviors and 21st century norms that pointed us in the direction of not just chronicling and examining the circumstances encountered. We also wanted to perform these tasks such that we could share the experiences and *lessons learned* with our children, grandchildren and others. Thus, our subsequent research and work to fully appreciate the relationship between behaviors, societal norms and a richer life began by capturing a simple, straight-forward definition by which all of us could truly grasp the essence of human behavior.

In the remainder of this chapter we will share with you a brief summary of our effort to capture a suitable school of thought by which all of us can comprehend the essence of human behavior --- and how behavior is affected by the influences of society. It soon became obvious that knowing the relationship between our behavioral tendencies and how we respond to circumstances in life is somewhat essential to influencing outcomes.

Our Human Behavior

According to the experts, human behavior comes in several flavors. Behaviors can be common, unusual, acceptable, or unacceptable. We, as humans, evaluate the acceptability of behavior by using societal norms. We regulate our behavior by means of societal control. For example, societal norms reward higher education with a larger paycheck; better decisions with more positive outcomes; outstanding job performance with a great career.

Human behavior is the result of attempts to satisfy certain needs. These needs may be simple to understand and easy to identify, such as the need for food and water. They also may be complex, such as the need for respect and acceptance.

Why do all of us act the way that we do? Why do some of us have an easy time, while others have a hard time adjusting to the ups and downs of life? As we can attest, finding the answers to these questions is not easy.

Our research revealed a whole branch of science and psychology wrestling with various classes of behaviors to answer such questions but has, to date, found no rigid answers. In general, you could say that you behave the way you do for a reason. However, the reason may not be clear. In fact, it may not be logical or rational either to you or to others.

One class of behavior called contingent behavior exists when each of your actions depend on what you expect others to do. Its role is apparent in your day to day behavior. The way you select what to wear to a gathering will depend on how you expect others to dress. You select the time and place that you eat lunch based on expectations of when and where others will eat. The road you take to work depends on what route you expect others to use. A student will decide whether or not to cut a class before a vacation based on how many other students he or she expects to cut the class.

By observing human behavior, you can gain the knowledge you need to better understand yourself and others. You can learn how you and others act and react under certain circumstances. You can learn how to identify the various types of behavior and needs of others. You can learn how to influence the behavior of others so that you can satisfy your own needs. You can also identify hidden opportunities and determine the paths to a more satisfying and prosperous life.

One way to reasonably detect and determine individual needs is by understanding the classic concept of basic human needs. According to the experts, we all have five basic levels of need. Most of our needs are in order of importance, such as the need to relieve pain is more important than the need to be liked by co-workers.

One straight-forward way to think about this idea is in this manner: *If you satisfy one level, then you work to satisfy the next level of need.* This *need* satisfaction is an ongoing behavior that determines your everyday thoughts and actions.

We found it beneficial to think of the five basic levels of needs and define them as follows:

SURVIVAL

The survival level consists of the basics we need to sustain life itself; for example, oxygen, food, water, sleep, and relief from pain.

SAFETY

The safety-security level involves the need for protection from possible threats, such as violence, disease or poverty. It also includes the need for the security of an adequate job and money in the bank.

SOCIAL

The social or belonging level addresses the need to be liked and wanted by family, friends, co-workers and others with whom we associate.

ESTEEM

> *The esteem level involves our feelings of importance. To satisfy our esteem needs, we must get a feeling of importance from two sources. First, we must have a feeling of importance that comes from within; this feeling is self-esteem. Second, since self-esteem alone will not satisfy our esteem needs, we must feel that other people believe we are important.*

SELF

> *Self or Self-actualization is the full realization of our own potential.*

These five levels of needs are acted out in human behaviors. When you understand your needs, you can help satisfy the needs of others which, in many cases may enrich your own life.

A Behavior Model

In order to better understand the basics of human behavior, we dedicated a substantial amount of time researching various schools of thought. The school of thought we chose to assist us is conceptualized in what we call a *generally accepted behavior model*. We have sketched out how we view this thought or concept in a diagram format in Figure 4-1. The intent is to share with you an important building block in our thinking as we thought through the development of the methodology we would use in our attempt to not just chronicle the life altering circumstances in our lives over the past thirty years but to also understand each event's contribution to our life's richness.

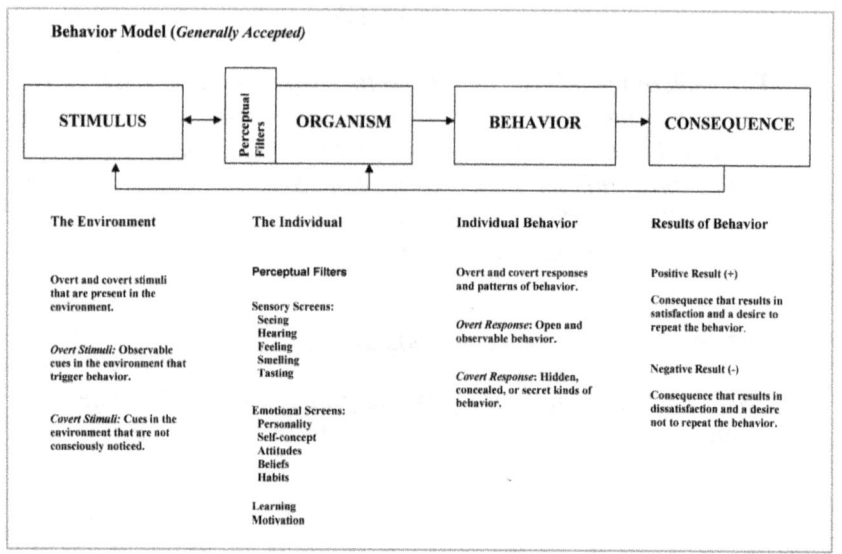

Figure 4-1 - Generally Accepted Behavior Model

According to this concept, there is a basic assumption that we all experience consequences in our lives as a result of our behaviors. When the result of the behavior is perceived to be positive [such as trying a new flavor of ice cream for the first time and liking it] the consequence results in your satisfaction and you naturally have a desire to repeat this experience in the future.

When the result of the behavior is perceived to be negative, such as having a terrible meal at a restaurant, the consequence results in your dissatisfaction and you have a desire to not repeat it.

Your individual behaviors and responses to life's circumstances contribute greatly to positive or negative consequences. These consequences may result in positive or negative outcomes in your life. If you change the behavior, you have a chance to change the outcome. So, how can you put yourself in the best position to alter your behavior and thus alter the outcome? It appears that based on the concept set forward in this generally accepted model of human behavior, you need to be more in control of two primary factors that contribute to how you respond and how you behave to life's circumstances.

The first factor is to be more in control of what are called *perceptual filters*. In this model perceptual filters are categorized into four classes: 1) Sensory Screens, 2) Emotional Screens, 3) Learning and 4) Motivation.

The second factor is to be more in control of the environment or more realistically, in control of the degree you allow your environment to affect how you behave. Your environment and your perceptual filters help to shape how you view the world. They influence how you view or perceive the situations you face and the possible outcomes surrounding your circumstances.

In Chapter 1, we explored in some detail the concept which set forth the idea that as we embrace each new day, we are also moving along the *Continuum of Life*. Inherent to the process of living, we all gain experience and insight which allow us to become more aware and therefore more in control of both our environment and our perceptual filters. It is this desire and ability to understand the societal and humanistic relationships that can enhance your ability to recognize and take full advantage of opportunities which can enrich your life.

Behaviors that Lead to Living a Richer Life

When we first started our journey, we surmised that there was a set of behaviors associated with living a richer life. Based on our personal and professional experiences, we initially developed the list of behaviors in Figure 4-2.

Ambitious	Dedicated	Dependable	Problem solver
Organized	Energetic	Responsible	Sense of urgency
Committed	Self-starter	Focused	People person

Figure 4-2 - Behaviors that Contribute to a Richer Life

However, as we expanded our research into the complexity of human behavior, we found that because of the composition of human behavioral process, there were significant underlying factors involved. We also learned that due to the interconnected nature of these factors and the varying possibilities of a resulting behavior, we could not simply identity a single set of behaviors associated with living a richer life.

Thus, we concluded that behaviors are too tightly aligned with and shaped by a set of underlying influences. These influences include assumptions, factors and intellectual preferences which have a tendency to change with time as we move along the *Continuum of Life*.

Figure 4-3 illustrates the underlying primary influences involved and how we view a common alignment.

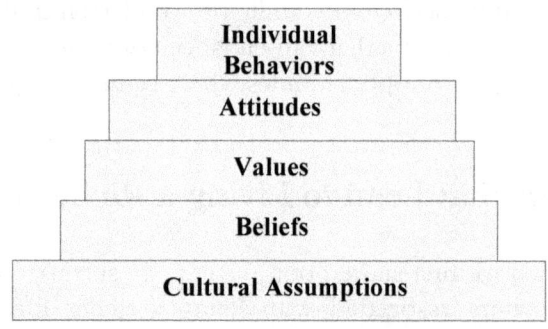

Figure 4-3 - Underlying Components to Individual Behaviors

Figure 4-4 presents how we characterize the underlying influences that contribute to shaping human behaviors.

Cultural Assumptions	The truth regarding our existence and our place in the world inherited and reinforced through indoctrination (usually at an early age) and based on the history and traditions of our predecessors.
Beliefs	An unquestioning view on how things should be and what is important based on our cultural assumptions and the 'truth' of our existence as a social being that we consciously or subconsciously buy into.
Values	A set of moral standards or rules (based on our beliefs) that govern the way we make judgments regarding the goodness or badness of factors in our environment and that influence what we set as the norms of a correct existence.
Attitudes	A stance we take and how we feel and what we think (based on our values) regarding situations and individuals and our interactions between the environment and other people.
Behaviors	The way we do or say things and the things we are prepared to do or say.

Figure 4-4 - Underlying Influences that Shape Behaviors

It appears that you must position yourself to acquire an accurate *view* or "snapshot" of where you are at any given point in time along the *Continuum of Life* in order to truly identify a specific set of behaviors which may lead you to a richer life. During this investigative process, you should ask yourself the following four questions:

- How do I view my existence or my place within the society I live in today [cultural assumptions];

- What is important to me now and what will be important to me in the future [beliefs];

- How do I currently view good and bad [values]; and

- What stance will I take regarding a circumstance if it happens today [attitudes]?

Our conclusions at this stage of our journey regarding human behavior and outcomes to circumstances can be summarized as follows:

- Behaviors which lead to a *richer life* are the behaviors *necessary* to facilitate the desired (positive) outcomes.

- The desired outcomes must be pre-determined by proactively evaluating and analyzing each unique circumstance based on a good *frame of reference* or model; and

- You must realize that your position along the *Continuum of Life* can result in a different outcome to the same circumstance at a different stage of your life. For this reason, you should not be afraid to do things differently or try something new.

CHAPTER FIVE

SPECIAL GIFTS AND OPPORTUNITIES OF CIRCUMSTANCE

"To give anything less than your best is to sacrifice the gift."
- **Steve Prefontaine**

"The people and circumstances around me do not make me what I am, they reveal who I am." - **Laura Schlessinger**

It was the fall of 1999 when we started our journey to chronicle and examine which of our gifts and our life's circumstances most significantly contributed to or diminished the richness that we experienced in our life over the past three decades. At that time, we thought we should first stand back and reflect on the true essence of life's gifts and circumstances. In this chapter we will share with you the results of our exploration. We also share some of our thoughts on both the wonder of human gifts in general and how we are all challenged mentally, physically, psychologically and spiritually when we must respond to life's changing circumstances.

We are sure that many of you have reflected on this topic from time to time. The emphasis of our investigation was to expose the significance of utilizing the individual gifts given to all of us at birth when responding to major events and circumstances. In our research we wanted to reveal the underlying foundation supporting how most of us initially respond. We knew that in order to properly examine the gifts and circumstances we had encountered over such a long period of time, we must first establish a mutually agreed upon appreciation for the roles that both gifts and circumstances may have played in our life.

Recognizing the Wonder of Human Gifts

According to some experts on the subject, what makes us human and identifies us as distinct from other creatures on earth is our capacity to manufacture the future. As humans, we have what seems like magical powers to transform our physical environment. The goals, dreams and aspirations that most of us create all flow from this capacity to make changes to our future. Other experts have deduced that memory, inspiration and talent are also unique *qualities* of humans. However, most agree that all of us are born with a unique set of human qualities or *gifts* that make us individuals. These gifts also serve to provide all of us with the instinctive skills and abilities to deal with life's day to day circumstances. These same gifts aid in preparing us for our future.

Your gifts are integrated into your sense of being. They come to you as natural as your sense of seeing, smelling, tasting, touching, and hearing. Figure 5-1 contains a list of just a few of the gifts that you may inherit at birth or that you innately possess in varying degrees:

Creativity	Critical thinking	Resilience	Motivation	Persistence
Humor	Endurance	Reliability	Enthusiasm	Honor
Self-discipline	Empathy	Leadership	Courage	Responsibility
Resourcefulness	Humility	Sympathy	Innovation	Fortitude
Spontaneity	Arrogance	Ambition	Integrity	Sense of humor

Figure 5-1 - Some Human Gifts and Qualities

These gifts serve as character traits. That is, behaviors which make a statement and send a message to others about *who you are* and *how you will normally respond* to a situation. Figure 5-2 presents a few examples of the messages that some gifts send.

Gift	Statement and Message
Fortitude	*"I have the strength to live by my convictions."*
Leadership	*"I am able to take charge and be a good example."*
Responsibility	*"I recognize my duty and honor it."*
Honor	*"I recognize the difference between right and wrong and act based on my beliefs."*
Integrity	*"My actions and decisions are guided by my values."*
Courage	*"I am willing to do what is difficult."*

Figure 5-2 - Messages Sent by Gifts and Qualities

Some of you *may not* have certain gifts to deploy while encountering life circumstances. Others may be armed with a full cadre of gifts to bring to bear. This is due to the fact that we are individuals and possess strengths in some *gifted areas* as compared to others. We all have often heard comments referring to someone as "a gifted baseball player" or "a gifted singer". This does not mean that others cannot play baseball or sing, to some degree. The inference is that some people possess innate skills and abilities that are above average.

After completing our research and following hours of collaboration, we concluded that four qualities appear to play the largest roles in critically examining and shaping responses to circumstances.

We found that the same four qualities or gifts can be significant contributors to your ability to determine which circumstances can become opportunities for life enrichment. These gifts, compared to others, more directly contribute to your ability to put yourself in a position to take the actions which will result in positive outcomes.

We refer to these four qualities as *Greater Gifts*. The *Greater Gifts* are exemplified by the following traits:

1) *Self-awareness*,
2) *Imagination*,
3) *Conscience*, and
4) *Independent Will*.

Self-awareness plays a critical role in your ability to examine your thinking and justly understand your motives as you encounter and respond to circumstances in life. If you are at a stage in life where you are financially secure and possess an abundance of self-esteem, you will tend to perceive the nature of a particular circumstance and the possible perils of the outcome much differently than if you have recently lost a major income source and find yourself physically and/or psychologically out of balance.

Imagination enables your ability to create in your mind a vision beyond the current circumstance which may be plaguing you. Imagination also allows you to visualize how certain outcomes can produce a different future depending on the actions you take in response to the circumstance today. When you encounter a life circumstance, the most dominant influence in your decision making process is the present. However, the actual manifestation of events associated with a positive or negative outcome to a circumstance lies beyond the present reality. Your ability to move the impact of a circumstance in the direction of a positive, long term outcome depends heavily on how you envision your future.

Conscience acts as your internal guiding system. It allows you to sense if you are acting with or against your principles. Circumstances are conditions that determine a course of action. Regardless of the magnitude or nature of the circumstances, they will have an impact on your life. Circumstances can serve as a valuable catalyst or means to enable you to move from one situation to another. Circumstances can assist you in enacting and realizing change in your life. Many life changes are necessary in order to put yourself on the course to reaping the rewards in life for which you are destined. Your conscience allows you to evaluate a circumstance based on personal principles [not solely on societal influences] and identify opportunities for life enrichment.

Independent Will gives you the capacity to act freely based on your own self-awareness and free from other influences. As discussed in Chapter 4, you regulate your behavior by means of societal controls. Research indicates that many of us tend to initially respond to circumstances in our life based on contingent behavior. That is, your actions depend on what others expect you to do. A strong independent will and the capacity to act freely based on your own self-awareness allows you to more thoroughly and open-mindedly evaluate the circumstances in life. An independent will also allow you to conduct a deeper search for opportunities that can enrich your life based on your own perception of need.

Greater Gifts can play a major role in your ability to maximize and get the most out of opportunities which may be embedded in life's circumstances. We observed the intrinsic potency and transformational potential of our gifts as both intriguing and powerful. Being aware of the areas in which all of us are truly gifted and focusing on developing our *Greater Gifts* is extremely important.

Responding to Life's Circumstances

Circumstances are conditions or facts that determine or must be considered in determining a course of action. Life's circumstances begin at birth and continue throughout your lifetime. Major events which spun circumstances can change your daily existence with an irregular heartbeat, a serious auto accident or the misfortune of being in the wrong place at the right time. Regardless of the magnitude or nature of circumstances, they can have an impact on your life.

On the other hand, it is also true that circumstances can serve as powerful catalysts in your life. They can assist you in enacting and realizing significant life changes. Life changes are often necessary to put you on the course to reaping the rewards in life for which you are destined. We are reminded of the advice given by legendary dramatist and prolific playwright, George Bernard Shaw, when he once advised: *"People are always blaming their circumstances for what they are. The people who get on in this world are the people who get up and look for the circumstances they want and if they can't find them, they make them."*

Based on our personal experience, we have seen how we have, at times, unconsciously forfeited our opportunities to control and alter the outcomes caused by major events which unexpectedly surface in our life. Many Americans from all walks of life do this, all too often, by *reacting* versus *responding* to the circumstances surrounding the event. They act as if it's an inevitable conclusion that we will suffer a periled consequence, lose something that is special to us or feel a certain way based on a particular set of circumstances.

Responding to events and circumstances in your life versus reacting is critical to any effort to take control and shape the eventual outcomes. Research indicates that when you simply "react" your way through potentially life altering events, you allow the circumstances at play to be in control of shaping outcomes. Many of us react purely on emotions or without a clear understanding of the present environment --- such as Who we are at this point in life? Who else will be affected by the outcome? What are other options?

When you simply react to major circumstances, you place yourself in a position to only accept the consequences [good or bad] which follows. You also run a high risk of accepting the same consequence and same negative outcome in the future.

As a result of responding, instead of reacting, you can direct your thoughts and emotions to a positive and constructive vision of the probable outcome. You can also eliminate much of the stress and uncertainty which may surround events.

Utilizing your *special gifts* and taking advantage of *opportunities of circumstance* can allow you to proactively shape positive outcomes to unexpected events in life and contribute to living a more abundant and richer life.

CHAPTER SIX

IDENTIFY OPPORTUNITIES AND LIVE A RICHER LIFE

"Nothing is more expensive than a missed opportunity."
– H. Jackson Brown, Jr.

Most of us would all agree that in order to succeed in life we must make good choices and select the correct paths. To accomplish this on a routine basis and with consistent outcomes, we need access to the knowledge necessary to closely examine each situation encountered as we travel along the *Continuum of Life*. By becoming knowledgeable, you can place yourself in a position where you are well acquainted with the facts, realities and opportunities surrounding the situation. From this position you are able to make better choices and select better paths. Thus, you are able to shape better outcomes and live a richer life.

This is also true when it comes to the process of identifying opportunities for life enrichment. The more you know about the details, particulars and the fine points surrounding an event in your life, the higher the probability that you will make the best choices and select the best paths available to you in response to the resulting circumstances.

As we began our journey, we first faced the challenge of recalling the actual details surrounding numerous events. It was somewhat easier to grasp details surrounding the handful of rare and unusual events. It was more difficult to recollect details surrounding events that surfaced more routinely. Because we were examining our life in retrospect, we knew exactly how we felt at the time and who was involved in each event. We also were able to recall the steps of the process we used to make final decisions as well as the specific actions that were taken at the time.

Of course, with this retrospective view, we were able to both identify those circumstances which turned out to be opportunities for life enrichment and examine the impact the actual outcomes had on our life. We are sure that you will notice the level of detail we were able to recollect, if you were to review the personal narratives associated with our life chronicle. We have incorporated four of the original narratives in Part III of this book.

However, you do not always know beforehand, as you travel along the *Continuum of Life*, which circumstances you should treat as routine and which circumstances to address more thoughtfully. Thus, sorting through the circumstances you encounter, in real time, to identify life enrichment opportunities requires a different approach. Understanding this as reality, we decided to address this dilemma by developing a methodology which could assist anyone in this process. To our delight, we were successful in documenting such a methodology as a part of this journey.

A Method for Identifying Life Enrichment Opportunities

As we began to map our approach to constructing the guidelines around the development of a method for identifying life enrichment opportunities, we quickly surmised that our approach must address a broader challenge, i.e. how to translate the principles comprised within the *Life Enrichment Continuum*™ paradigm into a useful tool which could be used to examine circumstances and identify opportunities.

One of the major guidelines we established for this new methodology was that it must have a broad application. In order to construct a methodology to be applied broadly, we would have to design it such that the range of attributes, influences and gifts associated with responding to circumstances were all appropriately recognized during the *opportunity identification, opportunity prioritization* and *opportunity examination* phases of the methodology. Within the methodology, there must be a procedure to reveal or *frame* our *state of mind* prior to attempting to identify opportunities embedded in the circumstance at hand and *prior* to entering into the opportunity examination phase.

Another major guideline established in the development process was that the *Framing Process* should include *"archetype-like generalizations" or standards*. Based on our observations, we strongly felt it was important that a deductive reasoning tool be used to prepare us to holistically examine each opportunity for potential life enrichment. This would ensure that we enter this phase with both compelling opportunities as well as the *"mind-set"* required to *prioritize* and *act* upon these opportunities. The ultimate objective, of course, is to generate positive outcomes that would enrich our lives.

As we began to map our approach to developing an opportunity identification methodology, we determined that the essence of the challenge could be summarized as follows:

A. How do we establish the criteria or set of attributes that can be applied to a list of circumstances in order to distinguish between *routine circumstances* and *circumstances which offer opportunity for adding richness* to our life or *minimize* any negative impact; and

B. Of the *circumstances identified*, as potential enrichment opportunities, how do we decide which opportunities have the highest probability to enrich our life *and* are consistent with our ability to realize them?

As we proceeded down this stage of our journey, we spent several months working through various processes and procedures that would provide a resolution to both Part A and Part B of this challenge. After narrowing the options down to a couple of approaches, we finally concluded our task by conceiving and developing what we named the *TWO-STEP Opportunity Identification Methodology*.

STEP ONE of the methodology included a technique to distinguish between *routine circumstances* and circumstances which offered the opportunity for adding richness to our life. We considered a routine circumstance as one that must be dealt with but whose impact would not significantly affect richness.

This step also posed a set of questions or queries to be used in *framing* or capturing our level of the self-awareness and our *mind-set* at the time the circumstances are first encountered. We named this component of the TWO-STEP Opportunity Identification Methodology, the *Framing Query*. We would utilize the *Framing Query* and the insight acquired as criteria to determine which circumstance presented opportunities for life enrichment.

STEP TWO of the methodology embodied a technique which identifies "available" and "actionable" opportunities for life enrichment and addressed Part B of the challenge. The goal here was to develop an approach that could be used broadly to assist in deciding which of the identified opportunities, from STEP ONE, would have the highest probability to enrich our life.

The obvious choice based on our research and our work up to this point, was to use the deductive guidance provided by the *Framing Query* during STEP ONE and augment this characterization with additional deductive reasoning to prioritize the opportunities. To aid in the prioritization process, we formulated a second set of questions that we believed would provide a sufficient degree of enlightenment when vetted or closely examined against each of the identified opportunities.

We named this set of questions the *Priority Query*. Figure 6-1 details the three probing questions included in the Priority Query.

> **Opportunity Priority Query**
>
> 1. *Do I have the physical, psychological & intellectual strength and stamina to take on what is required to move this situation, from where it is today, to where I envision it has to be, in order to obtain the value & richness I perceive it will add to my life, when fully realized?*
>
> 2. *Do I have or can I acquire the level of resources [financial, moral & spiritual] required to seize the opportunity?*
>
> 3. *If I decide to do nothing, am I ready to accept and live with the consequences that may arise as a result of this circumstance?*

Figure 6-1 - Questions that Embody the Opportunity Priority Query

Figure 6-2 shows a sketch illustrating the complete TWO-STEP Opportunity Identification Methodology, including all of its components.

The *Framing Elements* included in the illustration are essential components within the *Framing Process*. The Framing Process is where you can *figuratively* capture and honestly reveal the *state of mind* in which you find yourself at the time you encounter a circumstance. Our research led us to believe that the combination of the influences uniquely inherent to each of the Elements, either enhance your ability to use your natural gifts and better manage circumstances or prevent you from doing so.

The archetype-like generalizations which comprise the *Enrichment Platform* component are also essential to the Opportunity Identification Phase. The Enrichment Platforms serve as an aid to *optimize* the mind-set you have at the time the circumstance surfaces and enhance your ability to effectively *identify*, *prioritize* and *examine* enrichment opportunities.

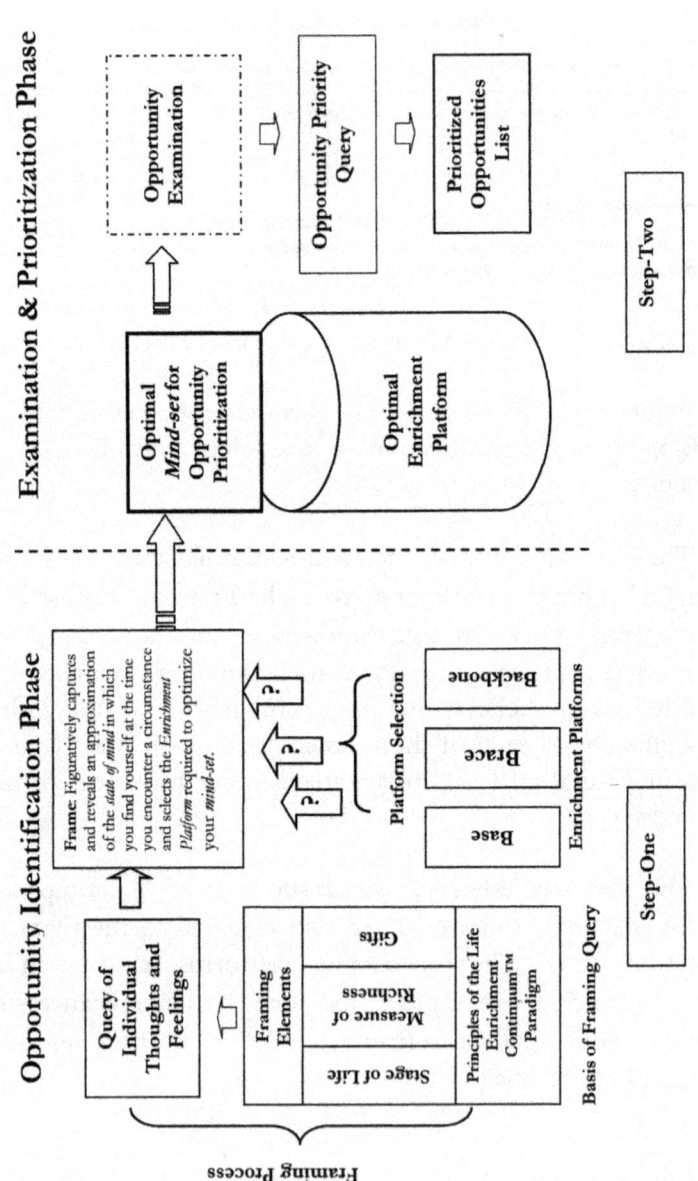

Figure 6-2 - Opportunity Identification Methodology

Opportunities and Life Enrichment

The insight we gained from our research and work in this area, in addition to the *lessons learned* from actually applying the modeling components presented in this chapter have proven to be invaluable. We believe that everyone should make an effort to discover those paths that will place them in positions where they are well acquainted with the facts, truths, and principles surrounding the events [and attending circumstances] they will face as they move along the *Continuum of Life*.

As we mentioned earlier and will repeat here, the circumstances of life begin at birth and continue throughout your lifetime. Sorting through, in real time, the circumstances you encounter on a daily basis in order to identify life enrichment opportunities require an approach which encompasses an appropriate level of desire, insight and methodology. Our research and use of the insights embodied in the *Life Enrichment Continuum*™ to examine our own life experiences have convinced us that the ability to live a richer life *truly lies within each of us*.

When it comes to the value of recognizing and taking advantage of opportunities, we are reminded here of the advice of Les Brown, the renowned motivational speaker and lecturer when he advised: *"If you view all the things that happen to you, both good and bad, as opportunities, then you operate out of a higher level of consciousness."*

PART II

A MODEL FOR LIVING A RICHER LIFE

"Most people can look back over the years and identify a time and place at which their lives changed significantly. Whether by accident or design, these are the moments when, because of a readiness within us and collaboration with events occurring around us, we are forced to seriously reappraise ourselves and the conditions under which we live and to make certain choices that will affect the rest of our lives."- **Frederick F. Flack**

CHAPTER SEVEN

USING MODELS TO IDENTIFY AND SEIZE OPPORTUNITIES

"A few observation(s) and much reasoning lead to error; many observations and a little reasoning (lead) to truth." - **Alexis Carrel**

"Reasoning draws a conclusion, but does not make the conclusion certain, unless the mind discovers it by the path of experience."
- **Roger Bacon**

Before we began our journey we established tangible objectives. The ultimate goal was to make sure we knew when we had crossed the finish line. The first objective was to systematically reflect and chronicle most of the memorable events and circumstances we had encountered over the past thirty years. Then, we wanted to be able to carefully examine the events to recall how we responded to the circumstances surrounding them as well as determine each event's impact [positive or negative] on our quality of life.

We quickly formulated a method by which we would break the three decades into five year increments. We then proceeded by recording each event and the circumstances surrounding it as succinctly as we could recall them. We decided to also place notes, alongside each major entry, detailing how we perceived the emotional, spiritual and financial aspects of our lives, as a couple and as individuals, during each incremental period.

After several months of recollection and dozens of entries, we found ourselves at the point where we needed to begin the mental chore of *reconstructing* how we approached and examined the circumstances surrounding each major event. Based on our rather logical nature [both being born under Aquarius and one day apart] we recalled that "habit" would have moved us to first explore each event and separate the *facts* from the *folklore*.

Then, we would have closely observed each situation seeking the options [changes required, decisions to be made, gifts that could be used, etc.] available to us so as to address the circumstances at hand. We both fondly remembered the circumstances which required us to spend countless hours [and many sleepless nights] probing for opportunities [possibility hidden in the circumstances] that would have allowed us to regain control of the situation and produce better outcomes. We also recalled that we somehow were able to discover [in most cases] ways to arrive at the proper mind-set, to acquire the courage and to ascertain the resources required to take the appropriate actions. As a result, we had lived most of our adult lives financially secure, emotionally stable and with a mutual feeling of completeness. On the other hand, we recalled, in hindsight, several decisions we would have made differently based on some difficult lessons we had learned over the years and after living through the setbacks we did suffer.

As we progressed through this *reconstruction* phase of our journey, we found ourselves overwhelmed with the daunting task of retrospectively examining the scores of circumstances that seemed to be multiplying with each update of the chronicle. In order to make reasonable progress, we were somewhat forced, at this point, to unearth a practical and realistic method to *reconstruct* or *model* the portion of our life which centered on *encountering major circumstances* and the *actions taken* to control the outcomes.

As we shared with you back in the introduction, when we started this journey, we had no idea that it would compel us to develop what would become an interactive *model* capable of aiding an individual's efforts to reveal and examine life enrichment opportunities. Nevertheless, as our growing interest in human behavior, the intrinsic value of our natural gifts and the composition of life's inevitable circumstances increased, so did our *hunger* for a better understanding of [or at least a good set of reasons for] the dynamics surrounding our natural ability to get the most out of each encounter.

In our efforts to *feed our hunger*, we balanced the remainder of the *reconstruction* phase of our journey with tasks associated with constructing the connective framework and the remaining components of a comprehensive model. You may have noticed this change within the discourse of prior chapters as we encountered the need to shape the vision set forth by the *Life Enrichment Continuum*™ paradigm and how we could not escape the excruciating development task associated with crafting the TWO-STEP *Opportunity Identification Methodology*.

Surprisingly, as a result of creating this systematic approach to *reconstructing* or *modeling* the road we had traveled in the past, we created a novel tool to assist us in strengthening our *self-awareness*, *mind-set* and *willingness* to use all of our gifts to proactively shape our responses to future encounters. Thus, we increased our probability to make better decisions, obtain more positive outcomes and live a richer, more abundant life.

We are delighted that the *Life Enrichment Continuum*™ evolved as a consequence of our focused use of deductive reasoning, our research of relevant topics and the hundreds of hours of collaboration with colleagues and friends. We are convinced that this innovative paradigm, as embodied within the *Life Enrichment Model*™, can provide the *additional insight, broader perspective* and *enhanced focus* we all require in order to diligently approach the life altering events and circumstances we encounter in our lives.

Before we conclude the discussion pertaining to the details of our journey and move into sharing several of the *personal narratives* from our chronicle, we would like to share with you the answer to the question we asked ourselves about three years into this project --- *Why a model?*

We take particular pride in being able to share our *lessons learned* with you via the *Life Enrichment Model*™. However, as we have mentioned several times now, it was never our goal to go down this path. Nonetheless, we soon became convinced that *interactive models* and *deductive reasoning* opens up a new method of exploring and revealing tradeoffs, uncertainties, options and sensitivities surrounding human actions --- such as encountering life circumstances. Hopefully, you will also become convinced.

Why a Model?

Creating a model was not a part of our objective when we started our journey. But, as fate would have it, we needed more structure and consistency in how we were examining the circumstances and attempting to identify embedded life enrichment opportunities. We turned to a couple of gifts that both of us have been blessed with --- our *logical way of observing relationships* and our uncanny ability to *apply both experience* and a *macro-perspective* to the reasoning process.

With one of us having spent decades as an engineer & corporate executive [designing everything from electronic equipment for the space shuttle to business strategies for operational support of complex pharmaceutical industry relationships] and the other having managed multimillion dollar financial investment portfolios and obtaining a PhD at age forty, we were familiar with bridging the gap between observations and the real world.

So, when we faced the challenge of finding an approach to systematically examining circumstances and life enrichment opportunities, we knew that we must first investigate all possible sources which might offer a solution. Based on our work in drafting the concepts and observations set forth within the *Life Enrichment*

Continuum™ paradigm, we immediately began to search for a type of system or building block we could use to personify the paradigm's *Principles* and *Challenges*.

We must admit that when we started our investigation, there were a number of questions regarding how to approach this type of emulation. There were also many details and facts regarding the discipline of determining mind-set that we did not know. However, there were a number of things that we did know. As it would turn out, it was the things we knew that surfaced as being most valuable in helping to make our search a short one.

First, we knew from our prior research and years of personal and professional experience in tackling tough human relations issues that we were not looking for a *panacea* or a magical solution that would provide accurate predictions or even reliable guesses. We knew that there were almost an infinite number of interrelated and individually unique factors [humanistic and environmental] involved when any of us first encounter a potentially life altering circumstance.

Secondly, we knew that the concepts and observations set forward within the *Life Enrichment Continuum*™ were not *rocket science*. In fact, most of the concepts and observations are fundamentally sound and generally accepted by many. However, most of us [for a number of different reasons] do not fully utilize or do not consider [in the proper context] the practical guidance and direction set forth by the paradigm when we encounter emotionally, physically and/or psychologically charged circumstances in our lives.

Lastly, we knew that after decades of being subjected to various psychological and type-defining tests [as a part of our long corporate careers], the idea of using archetypes to reveal an individual's probable perspective, attitude or mind-set, was somewhat common place.

Therefore, it did not take us long after we started our investigation to come across the idea of deploying the construct of an *interactive model* and the use of *deductive reasoning* techniques as a solution. This approach seemed to be an excellent method to characterize the concepts, observations and assumptions set forth in the *Life Enrichment Continuum*™ paradigm. The approach would also figuratively capture and reveal the most influential factors in play at the time we encounter and respond to a particular circumstance. Figure 7-1 is a general representation of how deductive reasoning may be applied to reveal insights and draw conclusions.

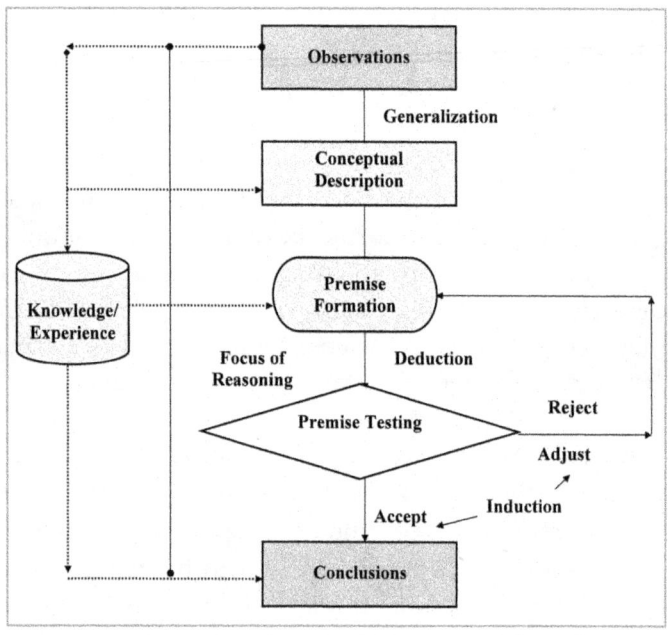

Figure 7-1 - General Representation of Deductive Model

In hindsight, it became even more intuitive to us as to *why a model* would be a good approach to addressing complex issues and situations in life.

Since a model is simply a collection of *parts* and their *relationships,* it can provide [based on assumptions] diverse views of an issue or situation. A model, when combined with deductive reasoning [logically working from the "general" to the "specific"] can surprise you, make you curious and lead to new questions. In Figure 7-2, we list several of the reasons that we came across that enlightened our understanding of why the use of models can be tremendously valuable in many situations.

WHY A MODEL?

- A model can be used to introduce specific content...such as knowledge, experience and guidance.

- A model can introduce us to important relationships that may not be obvious to us at a particular time ... such as when we are under stress or in unfamiliar territory.

- A model can provide an environment to explore relevant courses of action.

- A model can be used to explore sensitivity and variations ... even in human systems.

- A model can be used to explore "What-if" scenarios which allow us to weigh the options and understand consequences prior to making final decisions.

Figure 7-2 - Use of Models

The Life Enrichment Model™

When properly applied, the *Life Enrichment Model*™ can become an exceptional tool to aid in identifying unforeseen opportunities and determining the paths available to you as you encounter potentially life altering circumstances. The results of the model's queries can help you get into *the position* [both mentally and practically] to make better decisions, take appropriate actions and to more consciously make the adjustments required to formulate your responses to shape more positive outcomes.

The model's construct utilizes figurative depictions and characterizations to provide valuable insights into the intangibles in your life at the time you encounter a major circumstance. The depictions and characterizations are generalizations and should be used *as a guide* to steer you in a most probable direction. However, when you merge these *generalities* with your own timely [internal and external] observations and sound reasoning, this combination gives you a significant advantage as compared to simple *reacting* and *going it alone*.

When you provide honest and realistic responses to the model's queries and assumption-capturing techniques, it can become a significant complement to your own natural gifts and your efforts *to live a richer life*.

CHAPTER EIGHT

FRAMING MIND-SET AND ENHANCING PERSPECTIVE

"Everything we hear is an opinion, not a fact. Everything we see is a perspective, not the truth."- **Marcus Aurelius**

"The difference between a mountain and a molehill is your perspective." - **Al Neuharth**

Thoughts, feelings and actions don't have a mind of their own. They are all driven by perspective. According to the experts in the field, perspective is the ability to perceive things in their actual interrelations or comparative importance. As humans, we all have the ability to choose and shape our perspective on life --- and it doesn't have to be a mere reflection of the moment we are currently experiencing.

As our own life experiences indicate, it is important to harness the power of perspective and the perception of the richness in our lives, especially during times of duress.

In Chapter 1, we introduced the idea of viewing life as a continuum and the research which indicated that most Americans desire and aspire to be in the position to positively navigate the outcomes resulting from encounters with daily circumstances. In addition, we revealed the concepts of the *Life Enrichment Continuum*™ --- a paradigm which provides a systematic approach to characterizing the various environmental and human behavioral influences that come into play when any of us encounter circumstances in life. We also introduced the *Life Enrichment Model*™ as a practical tool which embodies the paradigm's Principles and Challenges.

While collaborating with several colleagues on the power of perspective and its ability to shape our perception of the major circumstances we face in life, we were reminded of the paradigm's Enrichment Challenge No. 4 which states, *"To enrich our lives to the fullest, we must not only recognize enrichment opportunities embedded within life altering circumstances, but we must also take the actions necessary to ensure that we fully realize as many positive outcomes as possible"*.

One of the most powerful and commanding actions you can take is to strive to plant yourself in the best position possible to identify and examine opportunities embedded within life altering circumstances. Our research indicates that your ability to position yourself for success [i.e. more positive outcomes and less negative outcomes] depends greatly on your perspective at the time you encounter a circumstance. This is particularly true when you find yourself in situations that are extremely stressful and psychologically challenging.

In the remaining sections of this chapter we bring to light what occurs, based on our research, when all of us initially encounter a potentially life altering event and how our perspective at that time shapes perceptions of the circumstances which surround it. We also discuss the internal and external factors that influence our perspective as well as how most of us perceive the levels of richness we desire in our lives.

We conclude this chapter by presenting the final juncture of our journey which necessitated the creation of deductive tools to accomplish our overall objective.

When Perspective Encounters Circumstance

Based on the experience gained over the last ten years from examining what happened when we came face-to-face with major circumstances, it appears that when *"perspective"* initially encounters *"circumstance"* the outcome produces, what we call, a *vectored consequence* i.e. one that embraces magnitude and direction.

In other words, to a significant degree, the initial *observations* and *perceptions* ascertained when we first encounter a major circumstance requires that we mentally frame the *difficulty of the challenge* at hand [magnitude] as well as the *course of action* we should take [direction] in response to the circumstance. The *consequence* produced during the initial encounter usually takes the form of being confronted with a set of captivating questions. The objective of this somewhat natural self-query is to gain some degree of situational clarity. Some probable questions and lingering thoughts that may surface are illustrated in Figure 8-1.

Questions That May Surface...	Thoughts You May Have...
How do I perceive the circumstance?	...*a threat or an opportunity.*
How do I feel about the circumstance?	...*full of stress or ready for action.*
How should I initially respond to this situation?	...*shoot from the hip or research my options.*
What form of action is required?	...*go it alone or involve others.*
How much time will this take?	...*too much time or it will take as long as it takes.*
How much will this cost me?	...*more than I have or the cost will be offset by the benefit.*

Figure 8-1 - Questions and Thoughts that may Surface.

The reaction that most of us have to such questions reveals our initial *perception* of the overall situation and shapes how we will subsequently perceive the nature and severity of the circumstance. This is due to the mind's propensity to register *initial thoughts* as the *truth or fact*.

Our research led us to conclude that, for most of us, our initial perception is *framed* by *who we are* in terms of our thoughts, emotions, self-esteem, financial security, natural gifts, relationships and expectations at that moment in time. Based on this assumption, if you encounter the same circumstance at a different time or stage in life [say at 40 years of age versus 20 or single versus married], you would most likely be presented with a different perception based on a different perspective of yourself at that time.

This concept is also set forth in the *Life Enrichment Continuum*™ and its Enrichment Principle No.1 which states: *"As we travel along the Continuum of Life, from one stage to the next, we accumulate insights and experiences which alter how we perceive ourselves, how we perceive others and how we respond to opportunities for life enrichment".*

Your perception of a particular situation establishes your mind-set and the *platform* from which you view the surrounding circumstances. This includes the challenges you expect to face, the options available to you and the parameters associated with the responses you should provide.

In addition, your initial perception mentally *sizes up* the perils associated with the circumstance and prepares you to either accept the perceived outcome or ignites the energy required to take the actions necessary to shape a different and more positive outcome.

As was noted in the quote by Al Neuharth at the beginning of this chapter, in many cases, *"the difference between a mountain and a molehill is your perspective".*

Internal and External Factors Shape Perspective

Most of us are not aware of the many *internal* and *external* factors that are at play during the initial encounter with unexpected circumstances. Those factors include societal culture, behavior patterns, educational level, decision-making skills and personal/professional relationships. Many of us are also not familiar with how these factors invade our consciousness and take on significant roles in *shaping* our perspective and *hardening* our initial perception. These internal and external factors are at work throughout your lifetime, influencing your self-esteem and how you perceive the level of richness you desire [or expect] in your life.

In order for us to complete our chronicle, we needed a methodology to recall and reveal our *state of mind* as we initially encountered major events and circumstances. The methodology we eventually embraced, as we concluded our search, incorporated the effects that these *internal* and *external factors* may have had on shaping our perspective --- and thus our initial perceptions. This methodology lead to the development of the two final components of the *Life Enrichment Model*™, now referred to as *Framing Elements* and the *Framing Process*. The Framing Elements are used within the Framing Process to approximate the effects of these factors and to figuratively and systematically capture representations of *state of mind*.

Capturing and Revealing State of Mind

The research, collaboration and deductive reasoning we had conducted during our search to identify possible approaches to capture and reveal our state of mind at the time we encountered each circumstance, culminated in the spring of 2005 with the development of a methodology we now refer to as *Framing*.

Most of us typically think of *framing* or *frames* as the underlying constructional system or structure that gives shape and strength. As we discussed in Chapter 1, as average Americans living in the 21st century, the most complete perspective most of us have of ourselves and of our life takes the form of a set of ideas, conditions and beliefs [either inherited or assumed]. The sum of which tends to characterize the factors involved in shaping our daily thoughts, perceptions, emotions, beliefs and expectations. As we stated at the beginning of this chapter, *your thoughts, feelings and actions don't have a mind of their own. They are all driven by your perspective.*

In addition to recent research, our decades of consciously and deeply observing contemporary American life revealed to us the possibility of the existence of an *underlying system* or *structure* which gives shape, strengthens and frames *who we are* and *what we think* at the time any of us encounter a major circumstance in life.

After compiling a list which contained dozens of probable *societal norms* and *capitalist-minded ideologies* i.e. philosophies, beliefs, principles which seemed to be good candidates for comprising such an underlying system or structure in America, we finally selected six structural components.

Following further analysis, it became apparent that this set of components, in tandem, could figuratively and effectively comprise such a system. These six components, when viewed both *literally* and *characteristically,* form an *underlying system* which constitutes the *social and economic* foundation for the *work ethic* and *dreams* of a vast majority of working Americans today.

Following several additional months of lively collaborations with an expanded set of colleagues, we completed the development of the methodology. We used the *Framing* methodology as embraced by the *Framing Process* to systematically approximate our *mind-set* at the time we faced the major circumstances documented in our chronicle.

We were extremely pleased with the results. Of course, we carefully treated the output of the *Framing Process* as figurative and directional. However, we consistently noticed that by having this additional insight as we examined circumstances allowed us to more clearly comprehend the decisions we made at the time. We also were able to more fully accept the reasoning and characterization associated with the state of mind approximations.

We surmised the school of thought and general thesis of the *Framing* methodology as follows:

"Your state of mind and perspective can be generally characterized by capturing an *inventory of your thoughts* surrounding six structural components, referred to as *Elements*. These *Elements* are believed to comprise an underlying system or structure that gives shape, strengthens and frames *who you are* and *what you are thinking* at the time you initially encounter a major circumstance in your life."

The six structural components or *Elements* selected to represent the underlying system or structure are:

- Self-awareness
- Education
- Decisions
- Relationships
- Career Success and
- Legacy

Figure 8-2 depicts the underlying system or structure that gives shape, strengthens and frames *who you are* and organizes your *theater of thought* at the time you encounter a major circumstance in life.

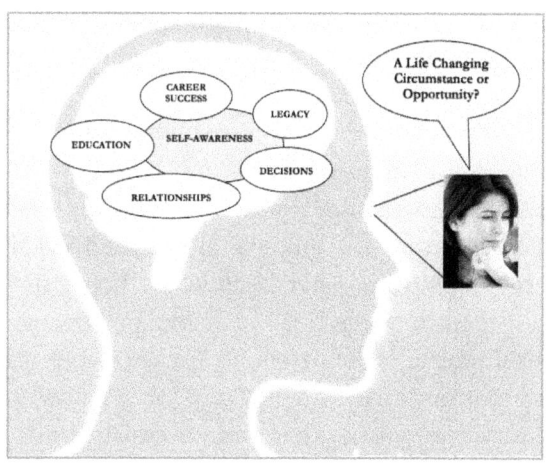

Figure 8-2 - Depiction of the Underlying Structure or Elements

During the application of the *Framing* methodology and the corresponding *Framing Process* to the events documented in our chronicle, we devised and answered a set of predetermined questions prior to identifying potential life enrichment opportunities that may have been embedded within the circumstances which surrounded each situation. This step of the examination process enabled the capture of the approximations associated with of the *mind-set* present during each initial encounter. We have subsequently included these pointed yet revealing questions, now referred to as the *Framing Query*, as a component of the *Life Enrichment Model*™.

In the final section of this chapter we describe the *Framing Process*. In addition, we present how it can be used within the *Life Enrichment Model*™ to figuratively approximate your *perspective* and thus your *mind-set* at the time you face major circumstances in your life.

The Framing Process

As mentioned in the prior section, we now refer to the *structural components* as *Elements* or *Framing Elements*. These Elements are broadly acknowledged in American society as fundamental to *survival*, *social acceptance* and *success*. Because of the pervasive nature of these Elements in American society and day-to-day life, all of us tend to keep one or more of these Elements as *top-of-mind* at all times.

When you encounter a major circumstance, the *Element* or *Elements* that are dominate in your *theater of thought* at that moment also *influence* your ability to acquire a *complete perspective* of the situation at hand. The Elements that are the least dominate tend to play a minor role [if any] in shaping your perspective. Putting yourself in the *best position* to gain a more *complete or balanced* perspective and to more extensively examine a circumstance for possible life enrichment opportunities, requires that you *optimize* or *augment* your theater of thought. The goal is to ensure that there is equal emphasis on all six of the state of mind *representations* as exemplified by the six Elements.

This concept is analogist with the common phase *"A car performs best when it is firing on all cylinders"*.

In other words, if prior to having your *perception* "hardened" by a partial perspective, you could *broaden your theater of thought* with additional insight and thus gain a more complete perspective. With a broader perspective you then can put yourself in a better position to more thoroughly understand the situation. Thus, possibly walk away with an initial perception and view of the situation capable of shaping a more positive outcome in both the near and long term.

Figure 8-3 presents the six Elements and the characterizations they represent within the *Framing Process* and the *Life Enrichment Model*™.

Element	Characterization
Self-Awareness	Who am I Now?
Education	What Can I Learn?
Decisions	What Happened Along the Way?
Relationships	Why Does Quality and Alignment Matter?
Career Success	When is Re-invention Par for the Course?
Legacy	Why Does it Come Back Ten-fold?

Figure 8-3 - The Six Framing Elements and Characterizations

By ensuring that the characterizations they represent all have a *"top-of-mind"* position in our thought process, the Elements can influence what you think, how you think and how you perceive the circumstances you are encountering. The *direction* [positive or negative] of the influence is determined by your ability to obtain, manage and recognize the personal and societal value associated with each Element. The *enormity* or *magnitude* of the influence is determined by the degree in which you submerge yourself in the chore of understanding how each Element and combination of Elements work to shape your perspective and add richness to your life. This level of understanding [or self-awareness] allows you to enhance your perception of situations, craft more targeted responses to circumstances and shape more positive outcomes.

As we discussed in Chapter 6, our research indicates that this is also true when it comes to the process of identifying opportunities for life enrichment. The more you know about the details, particulars and the fine points surrounding an event in your life, the higher the probability for you to make the best choices and select the best paths available to you in response to the resulting circumstances.

As we all come face-to-face with a major circumstance Enrichment Challenge No. 1 of the *Life Enrichment Continuum*™ reminds us to *"recognize life enrichment opportunities presented to us as we travel along the Continuum of Life and to leverage the experience, maturity and wisdom we have accumulated by shaping our behaviors, perceptions and responses in order to take advantage of these opportunities".*

Figure 8-4 illustrates the activities and steps associated within the *Framing Process*.

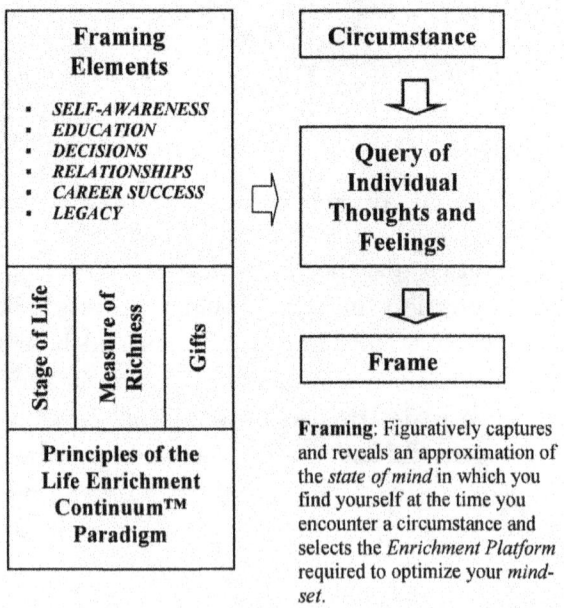

Figure 8-4 - Depiction of Framing Process

Chapters 9 through Chapter14 provide a brief description of each Element in terms of its structural and life enriching value in both your personal and professional life. These chapters also discuss the relationship between the Framing Elements and each Element's role in shaping how you initially perceive a potentially life altering circumstance.

For a deeper understanding and further personal or professional development, you should choose from the numerous articles, books and life coaching programs available in each of these topic areas.

CHAPTER NINE

WHO AM I NOW?
THE ELEMENT OF SELF-AWARENESS

"The truth is that our finest moments are most likely to occur when we are feeling deeply uncomfortable, unhappy, or unfulfilled. For it is only in such moments, propelled by our discomfort, that we are likely to step out of our ruts and start searching for different ways or truer answers." - **M. Scott Peck**

Thoughts on SELF-AWARENESS

According to many, self-awareness is where inner strength is discovered. We have learned through our life experiences, good and bad, that self-awareness is an enormously important life competency. It is truly one of the core competencies that needs to be developed most often and is most often overlooked. Self-awareness is largely a function of perception and observation. Self-awareness is one of the attributes of Emotional Intelligence and an important factor in achieving success.

As human beings, we all are complex and diverse. For us to become more self-aware, we must passionately embrace the need for understanding more about ourselves. An important part of self-awareness is recognition of the intrinsic value, not just of us but of others. Self-awareness involves becoming aware of who you really are and not just who you want to be. Self-awareness touches many areas of what makes you human. These areas include your habits, values, emotions, personality traits and the psychological needs that drive your behaviors. If you are conscious about your positive and negative behaviors and traits, you can more easily and critically sift through them. You can keep the good ones, while getting rid of anything that will hinder you from living a richer and more abundant life.

An important dimension of increasing self-awareness is the increase in your level of consciousness as well as your enhanced ability to connect to your feelings and actions. By accepting and understanding your thoughts and perceptions, you will have a clearer picture of who you are, what life means to you and what you must do to live a richer life. A clearer picture will help you in making wise and sound decisions as you build your career, raise your family, nurture friendships and live your life in general.

One of the first steps in changing or enriching your life is self-awareness. You cannot expect to change what you are not aware of. Self-awareness provides the clarity to choose whether you express emotions out love or express emotions out of reactions of fear. Self-awareness provides the possibility for you to catch yourself in that moment prior to doing something destructive or even thinking a negative thought. As discussed in Chapter 4, self-awareness is a means to identify your unconscious patterns and raise them in your consciousness so they can be changed. It is through self-awareness that you identify and change the underlying core beliefs that eliminate destructive behaviors, create happiness and increase the level of richness in your life.

Self-awareness also involves self-knowledge. The more you know about yourself, the more you learn to trust yourself and rely on your own judgment rather than the judgment of others. Knowing yourself is essential if you want to change your life for the better. It is similar to driving an automobile. While driving, you must be attentive of your foot on the accelerator and brake, your hand grip on the steering wheel and your attention to the oncoming traffic ahead as well as your surroundings. It is not until you know your automobile and how to maneuver it, will you be able to steer toward the intended direction smoothly and safely.

It is beneficial in many aspects of our lives to know *who we are now* [at this moment in time]. With self-awareness, it is easier for you to change careers, embrace new life styles and change your future based on where you currently reside. You can more effectively enrich your life when you know the direction you should go.

Self-awareness is developed through the practice of *observation* and *focus* --- focusing your attention and observing the details of your personality and behavior. A good place to start is for you to find a quiet place on a Sunday afternoon and began a journal which captures the answers to the following questions:

- What are my goals in life?

- What are the things and events that make me happy, as well as those that make me sad?

- What are my strengths and weaknesses?

- What are my values and beliefs?

- What is my philosophy of life?

- What are my achievements to date and how did I attain them?

- What are my failures?

- What caused the failures, as well as what can be done to prevent them?

- How do I relate with people?

- How do I deal with people, events, and things?

- How do I see myself and others?

Some of you may say that you do not need to take the time to write down the responses to such questions. You know the answers and they are safely stored away in your mind. However, you should remember that awareness of the mind and how to direct its thoughts, beliefs and emotions, opens new avenues of possibility. Your life becomes vastly different when you can openly and cheerfully communicate what's on your mind [even to yourself at times] and when you are the one directing your mind instead of letting *your mind* direct you.

"Who am I Now?

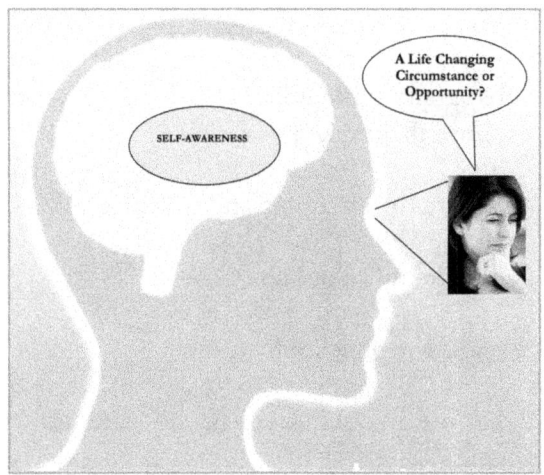

Figure 9-1 - SELF-AWARENESS as an Element within the Framing Process

SELF-AWARENESS and How We Perceive a Circumstance

"SELF-AWARENESS", as set forth within the *Life Enrichment Model*™, is the first of the Framing Elements which works in concert with other steps within the Framing Process to figuratively approximate your *perspective* and thus your *mind-set* at the time you face the major circumstances in your life. As an influencing agent, SELF-AWARENESS is characterized by the question *"Who am I Now?*

As illustrated in Figure 9-1, the Element of SELF-AWARENESS is at the core of the Framing Process and the Framing structure. When you come face-to-face with a major circumstance, your level of self-awareness and your level of consciousness regarding what's going on around you at this time determines to what degree you are able to target your energies and focus the appropriate skills and gifts in search of situational clarity.

In addition, the Element of SELF-AWARENESS serves as the conduit or channel between the other five framing elements i.e. DECISIONS, EDUCATION, RELATIONSHIPS, CAREER SUCCESS and LEGACY --- and the situation at hand. The level of your self-awareness at the time you encounter a circumstance is *directly in proportion* to your ability to ascertain a balanced perception of the situation as well as sustain a clear and complete view of the options to shape positive outcomes.

When the results of the Framing Query suggest that you should begin the opportunity identification process from the BASE Enrichment Platform, the archetypal character **Awareness Anchor** should be used to *optimize* or *augment* an incomplete perspective in order to ensure that the representation exemplified by the SELF-AWARENESS Element is *top-of-mind* as you initially encounter a major circumstance.

Figure 9-2 presents an excerpt from the **Awareness Anchor** archetype.

I am the *Awareness Anchor*. I am emotionally aware. I clearly recognize my emotions and their effects. I know which emotions I feel and why. I recognize how my feelings affect my performance. I have a guiding awareness of my values and goals. I know my strengths and limits.

I am aware of my strengths and weaknesses. I am reflective. I learn from my experiences. I am open to candid feedback, new perspectives, continuous learning, and self-development. I am able to show a sense of humor and perspective about myself.

Figure 9-2 - Excerpt from the SELF-AWARENESS Archetype

Figure 9-3 illustrates the influence that SELF-AWARENESS may have on your state of mind as characterized within the Framing Process.

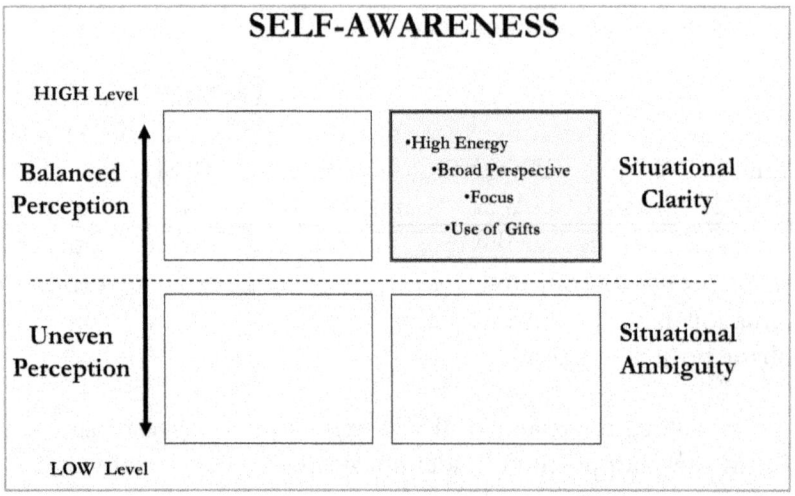

Figure 9-3 - The Influence of SELF-AWARENESS

CHAPTER TEN

WHAT CAN I LEARN?
THE ELEMENT OF EDUCATION

"Learning is a lifetime process, but there comes a time when we must stop adding and start updating." - **Robert Brault**

"The function of education is to teach one to think intensively and to think critically. Intelligence plus character - that is the goal of true education" - **Martin Luther King, Jr.**

Thoughts on EDUCATION

In today's world, a good education is essential. Not only will you be able to make better decisions in life, you will also be able to obtain higher paying jobs and respected careers with a good education. A good education helps you determine what is right and what is wrong.

Unless you keep your mind active by *learning*, you cannot fully benefit from the educational process. We have found that it is the combination of the educational process and continuous learning that gives all of us an advantage in many facets associated with living a richer life.

The ability to learn is one of the most outstanding human characteristics. According to experts, learning occurs continuously throughout our lifetime. The learning process allows you to acquire and expand upon knowledge, skills and insights which become instrumental in enhancing your ability to recognize opportunities that may be embedded in life altering circumstances.

Since learning is an individual process, you are more in control of what and how you learn than you realize. Many experts believe that all of us learn best from our own personal experiences. Consequently, what you learn and the knowledge you acquire cannot exist apart from who you are. With the realization that knowledge is a result of experience and no two people have had identical experiences, you can more easily understand why the same circumstance can be perceived differently by two different people [or the same person at two different stages in life]. Experiences gained as we travel along the *Continuum of Life* conditions us to respond to some things and to ignore others.

Learning also involves, in most cases, a change in attitude or behavior. As stated in Enrichment Principle No. 1 of the *Life Enrichment Continuum*™, *"As we travel along the continuum of life, from one stage to the next, we accumulate insights and experiences which alter how we perceive ourselves and how we perceive others…"* You learn to identify objects at an early age. When you become a teenager and become more aware of the impact that a good education will have on your life, you learn to improve your study habits. As you mature into an adult, you are presented with increasingly more challenging circumstances. Thus, you learn how to more effectively manage more difficult situations and problems.

Over the years, experts in the field have developed a number of theories in their attempts to explain how we all learn. Although psychologists and educators are not all on one accord, most do agree that learning may be explained by a combination of two basic approaches: *behaviorism* and *cognitive theory*.

In our research, we learned that distinct from behaviorism, the *cognitive theory* focuses on what is going on inside our mind. Most experts agree that learning is not just a change in behavior. It is also the change in the way you think, you understand, you feel and you perceive your world. On the other hand, experts view *behaviorism* as stressing the importance of having a particular form of behavior reinforced by someone, other than yourself, to shape or control what you learn. As we concluded in Chapter 4, behaviors are tightly aligned with and shaped by a set of underlying influences i.e. assumptions, factors and intellectual preferences. These influences have a tendency to change with time as we all move along the *Continuum of Life*.

A good education [along with life-long learning] not only teaches you the essential skills of the working world, it also prepares your mind to make sane, healthy and intelligent decisions about any situation you may encounter during your life's journey. As Gandhi once stated, *"Live as if you were to die tomorrow. Learn as if you were to live forever"*.

What Can I Learn?

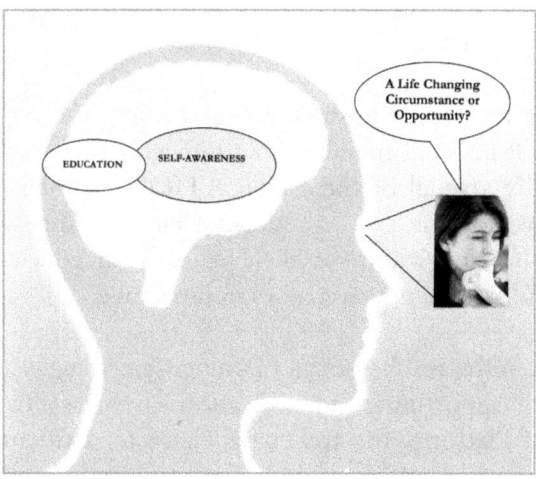

Figure 10-1 EDUCATION as an Element within the Framing Process

EDUCATION and How We Perceive a Circumstance

"EDUCATION", as set forth within the *Life Enrichment Model*™, is the second of the Framing Elements which contribute to how you internally process situations and establish an initial perception. As an influencing agent within the Framing Process, EDUCATION is characterized by the question *"What Can I Learn?"*

As illustrated in Figure 10-1, when you are faced with a potentially life altering event or circumstance, your state of mind or *mind-set* is ascertained through your level of *"self-awareness"* at the time. Within the Life Enrichment Model™, the EDUCATION Element couples with the Element of SELF-AWARENESS to ignite thoughts which compel you to ask the question *"What Can I Learn?"*

Our research and experience indicates that the level of formal and informal education you obtain along the *Continuum of Life*, combined with the degree to which you have developed your ability to leverage this knowledge, contributes greatly to influencing your perspective [what you see, think and feel] when encountering an unexpected circumstance.

Furthermore, a positive perception of your educational level at a given point in life, generally, is an indicator of a state of mind which has a healthy arsenal of the EDUCATION Element. Thus, a mental snapshot at the time you encounter a circumstance would reveal the assurance that you will most likely utilize your educational-based gifts while carefully examining a major circumstance.

When the results of the Framing Query suggest that you should begin the opportunity identification process from the BASE Enrichment Platform, the archetypal character **Education Enthusiast** should be used to *optimize* and *augment* an incomplete perspective in order to ensure that the representation exemplified by the EDUCATION Element is *top-of-mind* when you initially encounter a major circumstance.

Figure 10-2 presents an excerpt from the **Education Enthusiast** archetype.

I am the *Education Enthusiast*. I am aware of the demands of the global workplace. I know the needs of society are changing rapidly. I believe that education, being the knowledge of putting our potentials to maximum use, is key to a productive lifestyle in the 21st century.

I believe that education is more than collecting knowledge without understanding its value. I believe that the processing of knowledge fuels inspiration, visionary ambitions, creativity, motivation and my ability to bounce back from failure. I believe that we all gain true value of knowledge through life-long learning.

Figure 10-2 - Excerpt from the EDUCATION Archetype

Figure 10-3 illustrates the influence that the EDUCATION Element may have on your state of mind as characterized within the Framing Process.

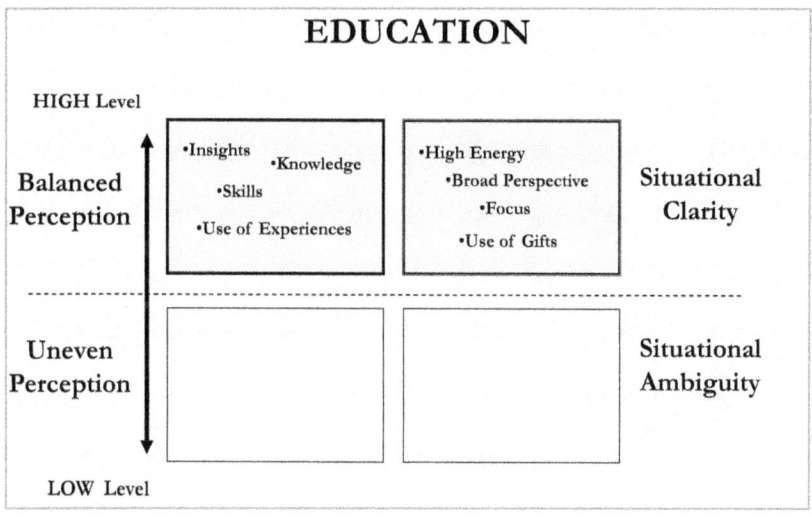

Figure 10-3 - The Influence of EDUCATION

CHAPTER ELEVEN

WHAT HAPPENED ALONG THE WAY?
THE ELEMENT OF DECISIONS

"The doors we open and close each day decide the lives we live."
-Flora Whittemore

"The hardest thing to learn in life is which bridge to cross and which to burn."
- David Russell

Thoughts on DECISIONS

How did you arrive at your present circumstance in life? What caused you to become what you are today? You might have been nudged along by your genetic code, pressed on by your natural inclinations, pressured by your peers, influenced by your environment and driven by psychological impulses. However, the "glue" we all use to shape our lives is the power of decision and choice. The path you have taken along the *Continuum of Life* is the result of the countless choices you have made on a daily, weekly, monthly and yearly basis.

Most experts agree that what distinguishes us from animals is our *free will*. In other words, as humans, we have the power of choice. Choice is a catalyst for change. Choice can lift us to amazing heights or fling us to desperate levels of despair. Such is the power of decision and choice. The decisions you make can bring you closer to or take you further from your dreams. The same decisions also can rob you of your ability to live a richer life.

According to our research, many of us act as if we were in rudderless boats drifting in the sea of life. We arrive wherever the currents and tides take us. Yet, most of us know that it does not have to be that way. You should understand that your destiny is shaped not by the circumstances that come your way, but by the decisions you make in response to encountering the initial circumstance. Thus, you should make sure that when you arrive at the point where you must encounter a major circumstance in life, you are aware of *"What happened along the way"*?

Many of us do not have this understanding. We avoid making choices that could improve and enrich our lives. In order for you to change your life you must first change how you respond to major circumstances in your life. To improve your life, you must improve the choices you make.

We have summarized in the following three steps some thoughts that may help you improve the choices you make as you encounter major circumstances in your life.

- **Know your choices and your options**. This is not as easy as it sounds. Because most of the time your mind is on autopilot. Instead of deciding whether to rise at the sound of the alarm or hit the snooze button, for example, you act automatically. You act by force of habit. If it is a good habit, it works in your favor and there is one less decision for you to make. However, if it is a bad habit you may fail to take advantage of life enrichment opportunities or to shape positive outcomes. Thus, you should persuade yourself to become aware of your choices and your options.

- **Analyze before you decide.** Before making a final decision, you should determine and carefully weigh the potential consequences, as they affect you and others. Then, honestly assess your ability [resources, skills and support], at this time, to follow through on the decision you make. Without the necessary follow through, the positive outcome you desire will most likely remain a dream.

- **Make a choice.** After analyzing the situation and your options, make a decision which selects the best option available. The failure to make a decision is choosing to allow the circumstance and/or others to decide for you.

Thankfully, we all have the power of choice in our hands. You can be decisive and decide to acknowledge that you, and no one else, are responsible for your life.

What Happened Along the Way?

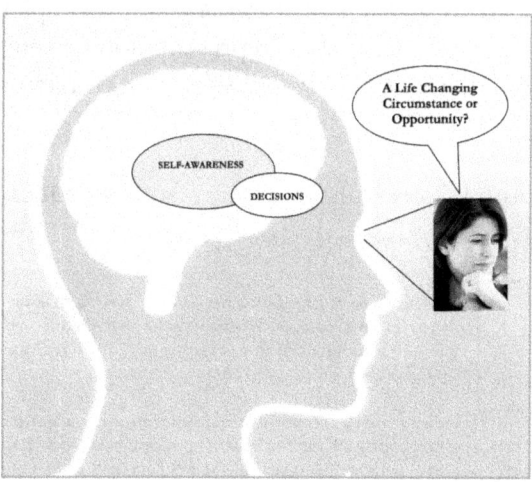

Figure 11-1 - DECISIONS as an Element in the Framing Process

DECISIONS and How We Perceive a Circumstance

DECISIONS as set forth within the *Life Enrichment Model*™, is the third of the Framing Elements which contribute to how you internally process situations and establish an initial perception. As an influencing agent within the Framing Process, DECISIONS is characterized by the question *"What happened along the way?"*

When you happen upon a potentially life altering event or circumstance, your state of mind or *mind-set* is ascertained through your level of "self-awareness" at the time. Within the *Life Enrichment Model*™, the DECISIONS Element couples with the Element of SELF-AWARENESS and reflects on prior decisions and prior outcomes. At the right moment, this type of reflection can lead to better decisions now and in the future.

When the results of the Framing Query suggest that you should begin the opportunity identification process from the BRACE Enrichment Platform, the archetypal character **Decisions Dynamo** should be used to *optimize* and *augment* an incomplete perspective in order to ensure that the representation exemplified by the DECISIONS Element is *top-of-mind* when you initially encounter a major circumstance.

Figure 11-2 presents an excerpt from the **Decisions Dynamo** archetype.

> I am the *Decisions Dynamo*. On my way to making good decisions I always list my options. It may appear that there is only one course of action, but I know that this is usually not true. Even if my situation seems limited, I always manage to identify alternatives.
>
> I always weigh the possible outcomes to every major circumstance in my life. For every possible course of action, I list all possible outcomes. I then label them as either having a positive or negative impact on the richness of my life. One method I use to track this analysis is to place a plus sign (+) next to each positive outcome and a minus sign (-) next to each negative outcome.
>
> I always consult my gift of intuition. If I am not gifted in an area which would help make a better decision, I will always seek input from someone I trust.

Figure 11-2 - Excerpt from the DECISIONS Archetype

Figure 11-3 illustrates the influence that DECISIONS may have on your state of mind as characterized within the Framing Process.

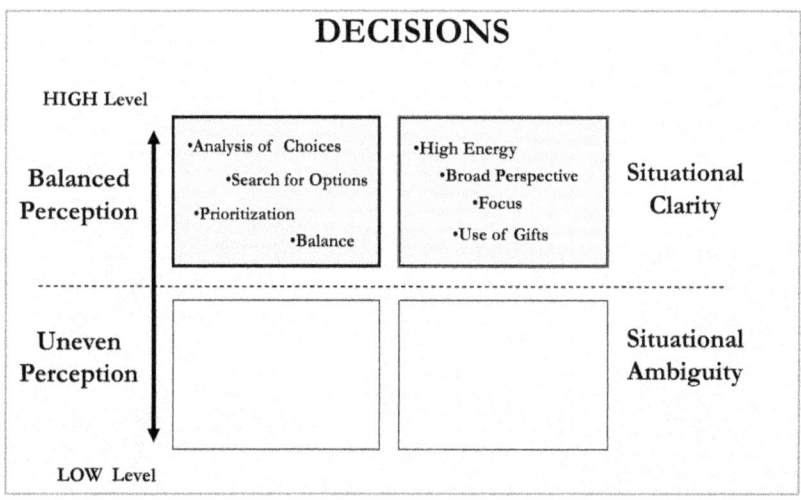

Figure 11-3 - The Influences of DECISIONS

CHAPTER TWELVE

WHY DOES QUALITY AND ALIGNMENT MATTER?
THE ELEMENT OF RELATIONSHIPS

"We talk about the quality of product and service. What about the quality of our relationships and the quality of our communications and the quality of our promises to each other?" - **Max de Pree**

"Treasure your relationships, not your possessions."
- **Anthony J. D'Angelo**

Thoughts on RELATIONSHIPS

When all of us reach the end of the *Continuum of Life*, it will not matter how successful we have been or how many assets we have accumulated. What will be important is that we have built meaningful relationships with people. In fact, a life is wasted if it has not had an impact on the lives of others.

We all crave for and certainly need social contact. Relationships are very important to us, whatever age, nationality or gender. All relationships are different. They come in as many shapes and sizes as there are human personalities. Without relationships, your life can become empty, boring and lonely. With, relationships, your life can be fun, fulfilling and sometimes stressful.

Relationships however, change and develop as you move along the *Continuum of Life* i.e. your relationships with your parents change as you move toward more independence and build closer relationships outside the family with your peers.

Relationships vary between different people and different groups. When you find yourself in the position of authority you expect others to obey you and do what you say. Friends expect you to offer support, encouragement and fun. This is also what you expect from them. The pace of life in 21st Century America is such that often some relationships are given a low priority on the list of things we all need to nourish on a daily basis. Over our thirty years together as a couple, we have learned that it is important that we both maintain quality relationships that are built on strong foundations.

When you encounter potentially life altering events and circumstances in life, your relationships often play an important role in influencing how you perceive and respond to the surrounding circumstances. As a result, if you allow the relationships in your life to steer you in a direction that is not consistent with those of life enrichment opportunities, you will not experience the positive outcomes required to live a more abundant and richer life. Quality relationships tend to generate positive outcomes.

One guideline that can be used to determine if you are in a quality relationship is your perceived level of satisfaction with the *value* you receive from the association. However, even within valued and long-lasting relationships, it is a good idea for you to conduct an honest and critical examination periodically. This should be the case with personal, professional as well as casual relationships. When conducting such an examination, one of the fundamental questions that you should ask is: *"How do I know if I am involved in a positive, mutually beneficial relationship?"*

In researching relationships and how they contribute to living a richer life, we developed a short list of what we call *Relationship Qualities*. None of the items on the list should be surprising. However, in our experience, when all five are present in personal and professional relationships, there is a higher probability of maintaining the kind of quality and potentially long-lasting relationship which contributes to living a richer life. Here is our list.

- **Communication** - Open two-way communication is a must. We cannot over emphasize the importance of communication. If you are not able to open up and talk about things, then the relationship has the potential to go astray. When you have something on your mind and let it go without discussing it, it usually surfaces elsewhere.

- **Honesty** - Be honest and expect honesty. Being honest and not lying is crucial to a good relationship. Even "half-truths" are not healthy for a quality relationship.

- **Trust** - Be trustful and be trustworthy. If you cannot trust a friend, a relative, a co-worker or a business partner, then difficulty looms.

- **Respect** - Be respectful and expect respect. A positive, quality relationship has a fundamental underpinning of mutual respect. It is okay to disagree but you must respect each other's opinions and differences.

- **Alignment** - In order to place yourself in the position to make good choices, better decisions and shape positive outcomes you must have relationships that are aligned with your interests and desires. Maintaining relations in your life that are "askew" and "misaligned" with your own goals and aspirations will drain you of the energy and the focus you need to tackle difficult circumstances.

Why Does Quality and Alignment Matter?

Figure 12-1 - RELATIONSHIPS as an Element in the Framing Process

RELATIONSHIPS and How We Perceive a Circumstance

"RELATIONSHIPS", as set forth within the *Life Enrichment Model*™, is the fourth of the Framing Elements which contribute to how you internally process situations and establish an initial perception. As an influencing agent within the Framing Process, RELATIONSHIPS is characterized by the question *"Why does quality and alignment matter?"*

When coming face-to-face with a potentially life altering event or circumstance, your state of mind or *mind-set* is ascertained through your level of "self-awareness" at the time. Within the Life Enrichment Model™, the RELATIONSHIP Element couples with the Element of SELF-AWARENESS to guide your efforts to ensure that the relationships in your life are aligned and supportive of what is required of you to adequately respond to life altering circumstances.

When the results of the Framing Query suggest that you should begin the opportunity identification process from the BRACE Enrichment Platform, the archetypal character **Relationship Rancher** should be used to *optimize* and *augment* an incomplete perspective in order to ensure that the representation exemplified by the RELATIONSHIPS Element is *top-of-mind* when you initially encounter a major circumstance.

Figure 12-2 presents an excerpt from the **Relationship Rancher** archetype.

I am the ***Relationship Rancher***. There are many qualities that make up positive and valuable relationships. Good support, compromise and honest communication are just a few of the qualities I desire in all of my relationships. I believe in creating value in my life and contributing value to others.

My definition of value in a relationship includes the ability to grow, leverage and mutually benefit from the association. It also includes a balance between the ups and downs while expecting significantly more positives than negatives. I have learned that in order to grow, leverage and maintain positive, valuable relationships, I must first focus on developing my own relationship skills.

Figure 12-2 - An Excerpt from the Relationship Rancher Archetype

Figure 12-3 illustrates the influence that RELATIONSHIPS may have on your state of mind as characterized within the Framing Process.

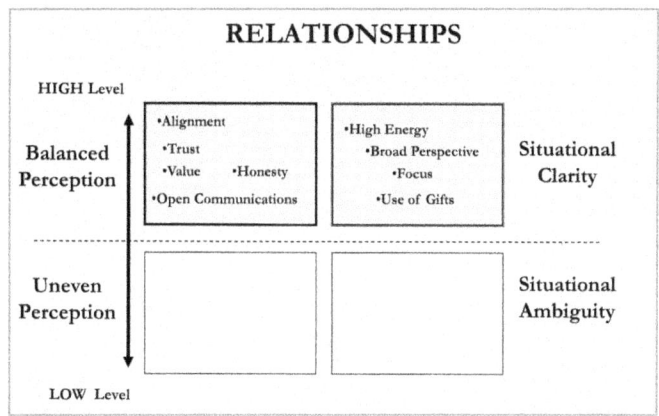

Figure 12-3 - The Influence of RELATIONSHIPS

CHAPTER THIRTEEN

WHEN IS RE-INVENTION PAR FOR THE COURSE? THE ELEMENT OF CAREER SUCCESS

"When you are inspired by some great purpose, some extraordinary project, all your thoughts break their bounds. Your mind transcends limitations, your consciousness expands in every direction and you find yourself in a new, great and wonderful world. Dormant forces, faculties and talents become alive, and you discover yourself to be a greater person by far than you ever dreamed yourself to be." - **Patanjali**

Thoughts on CAREER SUCCESS

As mentioned in Chapter 5, if you are at a stage in life where you are financially secure and possess an abundance of self-esteem, you will tend to perceive the nature of a particular circumstance and the possible perils of the outcome much differently than if you have recently lost a major source of income and find yourself physically or psychologically out of balance.

Career success plays a major role in American society in cultivating your ability to become financially secure, possess an abundance of self-esteem and maintain the balance required to live a truly richer life. However, our research revealed that many of us do not have a clear definition of what career success means in our life. Thus, it is important to keep a clear definition of career success top-of-mind by asking yourself, *How do I define career success at this stage of life?*

Why is this question important? Well, one of the most core activities in today's shifting world economy is getting a good grasp on your own definition or model of success. This is important for a number of reasons. First, if you have not done this, you do not know what is best for you. Secondly, it is impossible to make the best career decisions if you do not have an individual and honest view of how you define success…during all stages of your life.

Thirdly, you cannot reach your level of self-actualization until you know the level of success it encompasses. If you have a clear understanding of where you are on your current career path as well as a clear definition of success, you will be in a better position to identify embedded opportunities and to shape more positive outcomes when confronted with major circumstances.

Because of the impact that career success has on your quality of life [and your ability to live a more abundant and richer life] having a clear definition, as it relates to your attainment, is always relevant. There is never a bad time to discover and update your definition of career success and what it takes to at least *shoot par*…the golf score indicating no pluses yet no minuses.

Today's economic realities make the timing of such a discovery even more critical. If your career hasn't gone according to plan maybe it's time to *re-invent* yourself or move in another direction in order to place yourself in a position to at least *shoot par or better*. However, even if you are one of the fortunate ones whose career has stayed on track, it is always prudent to re-examine what it is you actually want from a career during another stage of life.

Even though many of you may not have taken the time to document your sense of career success, it has already been defined by where you presently find yourself in life. You are already subconsciously following a model of career and life success. The question is whether the model is your own or one that you inherited. One of your greatest career challenges is identifying goals and definitions of success that are true to your own desires and expectations rather than ones you may have inherited from family, society and other outside forces. If you follow a path to success that isn't your own, you may achieve your goals, but when you arrive at your destination, you may not feel as successful or as fulfilled as you anticipated.

Throughout our life, we have found it helpful to clearly understand the assumptions we have made regarding our career [and life] success and to question them based on our current circumstances. All of us have what it takes to reaffirm our existing models or adopt new models and re-invent ourselves for success. All it takes is some honest thinking, clarity of purpose and the discipline to stay true to our values.

We have found the following approach to be helpful during the career and life-planning activities we have undertaken over the years:

- **Accept that there are always other options**. There have never been more options or valid ways of defining career and life success as in America today.

- **Examine career paths**. Do you love what you do? Do you do extraordinary work as a result? Does your work complement your personal and family life or detract from it? Are you excited about your vision of the future? Is this the best use of your precious gifts and time?

- **Create some quiet, introspective time**. Ask yourself these questions: What makes me happy? How do I feel? What do I want?

When Is Re-Invention Par For The Course?

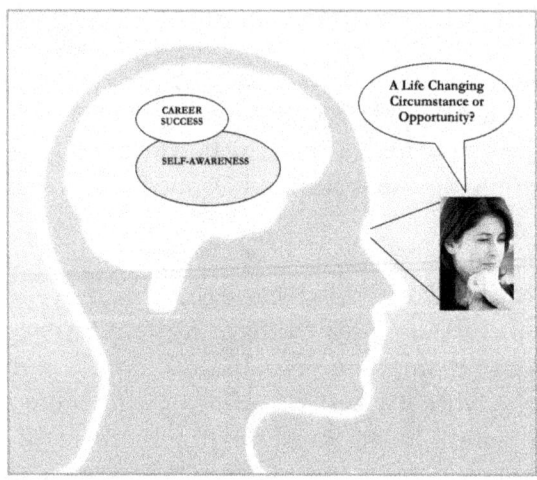

Figure 13-1 - CAREER SUCCESS as an Element in the Framing Process

CAREER SUCCESS and How We Perceive a Circumstance

"CAREER SUCCESS", as set forth within the Life Enrichment Model™, is the fifth of the Framing Elements which contribute how we internally process situations and establish an initial perception. As an influencing agent within the Framing Process, CAREER SUCCESS is characterized by the question *"When is re-invention par for the course?*

When you encounter a potentially life altering event or circumstance, your state of mind or *mind-set* is ascertained through your level of "self-awareness" at the time. Within the Life Enrichment Model™, the CAREER SUCCESS Element couples with the Element of SELF-AWARENESS to ignite a thoughtful review of how the response to the circumstance at hand can benefit or be benefited by your current and/or future level of career success.

When the results of the Framing Query suggest that you should begin the opportunity identification process from the BACKBONE Enrichment Platform, the archetypal character **Career Carver** is used to *optimize* and *augment* an incomplete perspective in order to ensure that the representation exemplified by the CAREER SUCCESS Element is *top-of-mind* when you initially encounter a major circumstance. Figure 13-2 presents an excerpt from the **Career Carver** archetype.

> I am **Career Carver**. I know that in America today, more than ever, I am responsible for building my career and guiding it to the level of success that complements the richness I desire in my life.
>
> I am a life-long learner. I know that one of the major factors for career success is to never stop learning. I know that my world is constantly changing and that just as in life, career success depends on identifying new ways of doing things. I know that in order to keep my career on track, I must continuously update my skills and knowledge.

Figure 13-2 - An Excerpt from the Career Carver Archetype

Figure 13-3 illustrates the influence that CAREER SUCCESS may have on your state of mind as characterized within the Framing Process.

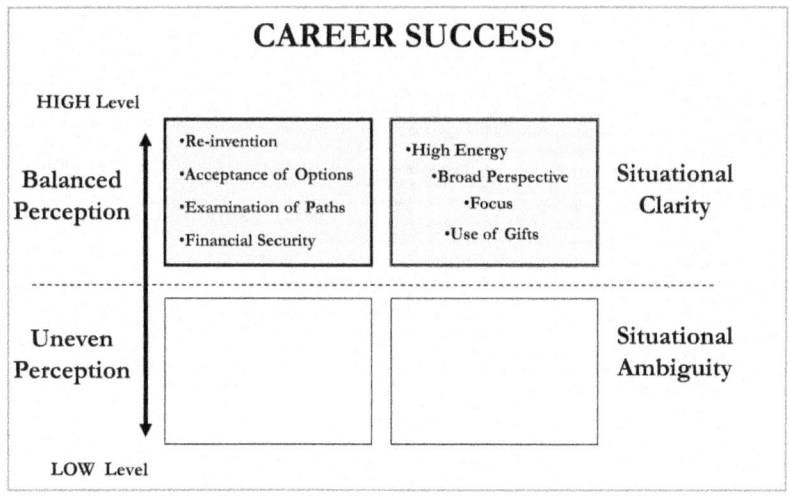

Figure 13-3 - The Influence of CAREER SUCCESS

CHAPTER FOURTEEN

WHY DOES IT COME BACK TEN-FOLD?
THE ELEMENT OF LEGACY

"The meaning of life is to find your gift; the purpose of life is to give it away". - **Joy J. Golliver**

"No person was ever honored for what he (or she) received. Honor has been the reward for what he (or she) gave." - **Calvin Coolidge**

Thoughts on LEGACY

When all of us go through life we subscribe to different value systems. Some of us place much emphasis on being financially secure. Others of us consider relationships to be more important than everything else. There are those of us who consider outward appearance and making a good impression to be the most important possessions, sometimes without considering the cardinal principles of character.

These are some of the differences in the perspectives through which most of us view life and things that are important to us as we travel along life's continuum. However, as we discussed in Chapter 4, as you move along the *Continuum of Life* and achieve earthly success there is a yearning to satisfy a higher level of need beyond self or self-actualization. Many of us satisfy this need by leaving a richer legacy.

Recent history indicates that most of the time the difference between prosperous nations and failed states, affluent societies and struggling ones, rich people and poor people is in their desire to leave lasting legacies. One group focuses on leaving valuable skills, ideals and values to the coming generations where the other is only concerned with gratifying their present desires. This group is described as having a tendency to sacrifice tomorrow for instant gratification today.

When you choose to leave a legacy you take a futuristic approach to life. This is a focus that goes beyond your period of existence here on earth. With this approach you concern yourself with how the next generation of youth will benefit from your existence on earth after you are gone. Taking this approach to life does not require special skills but a conscious decision to live a life with a desire to leave a lasting legacy.

In the context of living a richer life, creating a lasting legacy is not a one-time task. It is built through the steady accumulation and sharing of wealth and a constant life performance which epitomizes excellence. Your legacy is something that you leave for future generations.

None of us can honestly start out inventing our legacy. Rather, we are all *"who we are"* and we do *"what we do"*. The world notices and assigns to us the definition of our legacy. The best legacies are innocent consequences of a life lived well.

Here are a few reasons why we believe a legacy is important:

- The legacy you leave is part of the ongoing foundations of life. Those who came before you left the world you live in. Those who will come after will have only what you leave them.

- Legacies tend to have power for good and for bad. There are people who have changed the world for good, people who have opened up new worlds for millions of others, people who have spurred others onto new heights. There are parents who have blessed their children with greatness and other parents who have ruined their children's fragile minds and hearts.

- Leaving a legacy is an act of responsibility. Because of the power of your life and the legacies you leave, it is a great responsibility to choose to leave a positive legacy. We believe that part of living a richer life includes the goal of leaving a legacy.

- Purposefully leaving a legacy for others breaks the downward pull of selfishness that can be inherent in all of us. When you strive to leave a legacy, you are acting with a selflessness that can only be good for all of humanity.

- Being mindful of leaving a legacy keeps you focused on the bigger picture. Legacy building requires a long view of the future.

It has been our experience that when we give freely and without any expectations of a return, the act of giving itself reinforces who we are as human beings. Yet, we have also experienced time and time again that what we have unconditionally given to family, friends and others has come back to us ten-fold…in many forms…and has enriched our lives.

Why Does it Come Back Ten-fold?

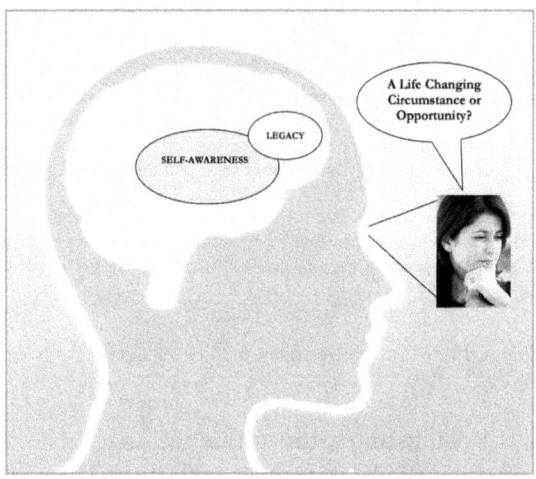

Figure 14.1 - LEGACY as an Element in the Framing Process

LEGACY and How We View a Circumstance

"LEGACY", as set forth within the Life Enrichment Model™, is the sixth of the Framing Elements which contribute to how you internally process situations and establish an initial perception. As an influencing agent within the Framing Process, LEGACY is characterized by the question *"Why does it come back ten-fold?"*

When we encounter a potentially life altering event or circumstance our state of mind or *mind-set* is ascertained through our level of "self-awareness" at the time. Within the Life Enrichment Model™, the LEGACY Element couples with the Element of SELF-AWARENESS to ignite thoughts which compel you to consider how your response to the circumstance may be viewed as part of your legacy.

When the results of the Framing Query suggest that you should begin the opportunity identification process from the BACKBONE Enrichment Platform, the archetypal character **Legacy Leaver** should be used to *optimize* and *augment* an incomplete perspective in order to ensure that the representation exemplified by the LEGACY Element is *top-of-mind* when you initially encounter a major circumstance.

Figure 14-2 presents an excerpt from the **Legacy Leaver** archetype.

> I am *Legacy Leaver*. I know that the key to success is to always start everything you do with an end in mind. I realize that this simple bit of common sense could really be applied to all aspects of life, including career, family, personal relationships and professional goals.
>
> I believe that to live a life of passion and significance requires making noteworthy strives and achievements. Our living should always express our personal values. As a legacy leaver, I express my personal values by integrating my charitable, family and financial goals.

Figure 14-2 - An Excerpt from the Legacy Leaver Archetype

Figure 14-3 illustrates the influence that LEGACY may have on your state of mind as characterized within the Framing Process.

LEGACY

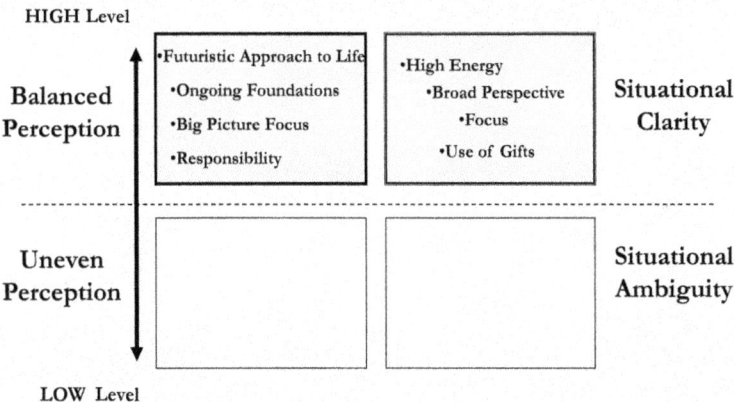

Figure 14-3 - The Influence of LEGACY

CHAPTER FIFTEEN

A MODEL FOR LIVING A RICHER LIFE

"Opportunity is missed by most people because it is dressed in overalls and looks like work." -**Thomas A. Edison**

To this point, we have introduced most of the components of the *Life Enrichment Model*™. We were somewhat compelled to develop these components to facilitate the recognition, examination and analysis of the scores of events and circumstances uncovered during our journey to reflect on the memorable events in our life together over the past thirty years. Our goal, of course, was to understand the positive and negative impacts to our life as a result of how well we managed each circumstance.

In this Chapter, for the first time, we provide an overview of all of the components of the *Life Enrichment Model*™ and the five stages which comprise the model's construct. We will also introduce the school of thought behind the *Enrichment Examination* process.

The overview is presented in two distinct parts.

First, we present a graphical presentation of the model and the sequence by which the model components are deployed within each stage. In addition, we highlight the figurative and deductive inputs and outputs of each stage of the *Life Enrichment Model*™.

Secondly, we provide a more detailed description of each of the model components and their role in the modeling process. This includes a key component of the *Enrichment Examination* process called *Modal Exploration*.

Part IV, *"Navigating The Life Enrichment Model™"*, contains an Application Guide. The guide can be used to apply the model to a potentially life altering event or situation you may be encountering in your life. It is structured to walk you through each of the five stages of the model and aid you in navigating the model's components.

The Life Enrichment Model™

The Figure 15-1 presents a graphical presentation of the *Life Enrichment Model*™, its five stages and the sequential flow of all of the model components.

During certain stages, the *Life Enrichment Model*™ constructively provides you figurative depictions and characterizations of the intangibles [such as state of mind, behavioral tendencies and emotional conditions] in your life at the time you encounter a major circumstance. The depictions and characterizations are generalizations and should to be used *as a guide* to steer you in the best direction. When you merge these *generalities* with your own timely [internal and external] observations and sound reasoning, this combination gives you a significant advantage as compared to simply *reacting* and *going it alone*.

The *Life Enrichment Model*™ can become an exceptional tool to aid you in identifying hidden opportunities and determining the paths available to you which have the potential of leading to a more satisfying and richer life.

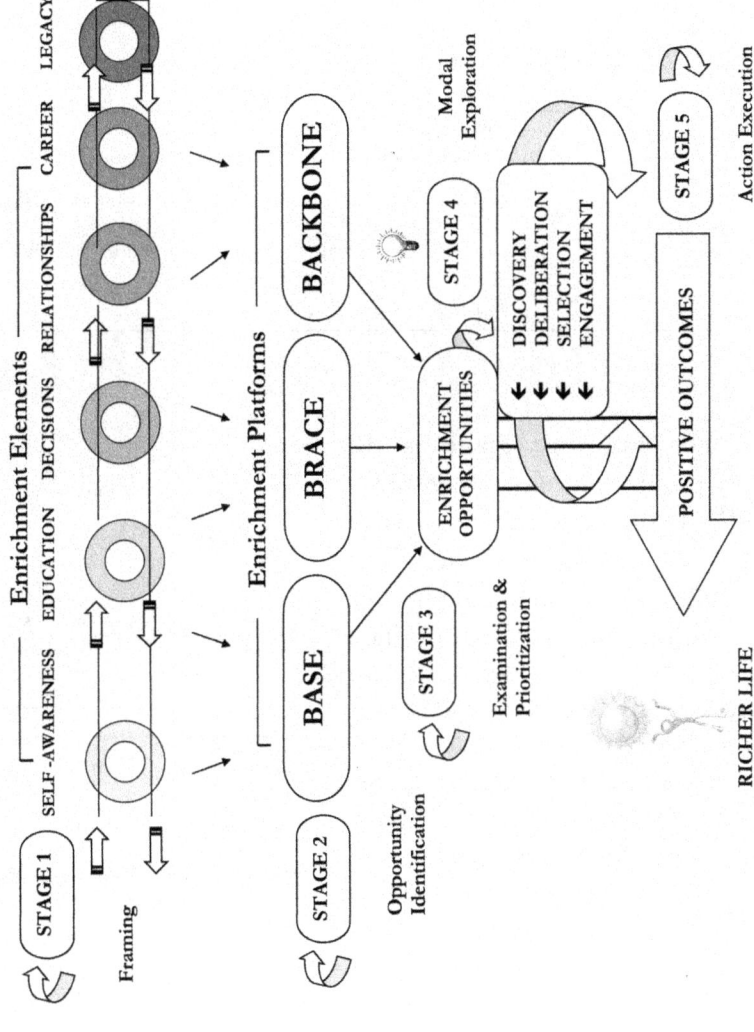

Figure 15-1 - Graphical Presentation of the Life Enrichment Model™

The Life Enrichment Model™ Components

This section presents the five stages of the *Life Enrichment Model™* as well as detailed descriptions of each model component and its role in the modeling process.

I. THE FRAMING STAGE

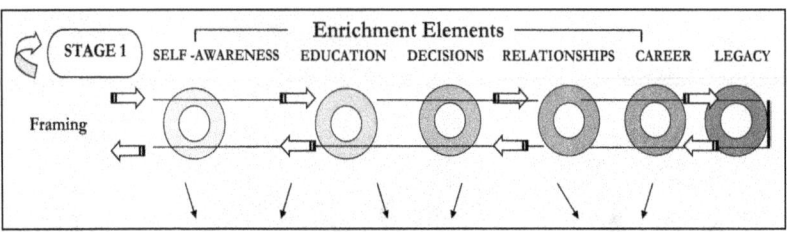

Figure 15-2 - Framing

The **Framing Stage** is the first step in the *Life Enrichment Model™*. In this stage the goal is to extract a view or *frame* of your *mind-set* in order to reveal how you can place yourself in the best position [mentally] to identify and examine opportunities embedded within life altering circumstances. The modeling components used to perform this step are the *Framing Process, Framing Elements* and the *Framing Query*.

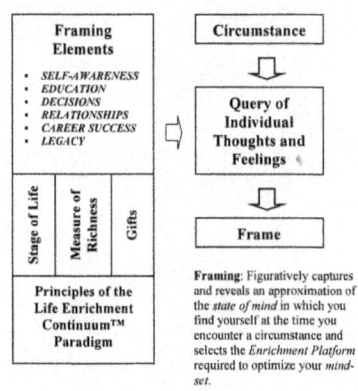

Figure 15-3 - The Framing Process

The Framing Process uses the Framing Query and the Framing Elements to aid in determining the "probable mind-set" present when you first encounter major events. Figure 15-3 details the activity associated with the Framing Process. The output of the Framing Process is an approximation of your *perspective* at that time. It is believed that this *approximation* is consistent with the "probable mind-set" you will take into the encounter. The *mind-set* you take into an encounter can influence what you think, how you think and how you perceive the surrounding circumstances.

The primary focus of the Framing Stage is to ensure that the representation exemplified by the Framing Elements all have a "top-of-mind" position in your perspective prior to moving into the *Opportunity and Identification* Stage of the model. This is achieved by *optimizing* or augmenting your mind-set with the representation set forth by the *Platform Archetypes*.

This optimization allows you to enhance your perception of the situation, craft a more targeted response to the circumstance and shape more positive outcomes. Figure 15-4 outlines the Enrichment Platforms and presents a description of the *Platform Archetypes*.

Enrichment Platform	Structural Focus	Target of Mind-set Optimization	Archetypal Character
BASE	Foundational Elements	Strengthens sense of "who we are" and "what we can learn"	· Awareness Anchor · Education Enthusiast
BRACE	Supportive Elements	Strengthens sense of "what happened along the way" and "why quality and alignment matter"	· Decisions Dynamo · Relationship Rancher
BACKBONE	Core Elements	Strengthens sense of "re-invention is par for the course" and "it comes back ten-fold"	· Career Carver · Legacy Leaver

Figure 15-4 - Enrichment Platforms and Archetypes

The Framing Stage's output is an enhanced *perspective* optimized to obtain a broader and more concise perception of the event being encountered.

II. THE OPPORTUNITY IDENTIFICATION STAGE

The **Opportunity Identification Stage** is the second step in the *Life Enrichment Model*™. In this stage the goal is to develop an initial list of circumstances which appear to have surfaced as a result of the situation at hand. The goal is to evaluate each circumstance to identify embedded opportunities and then analyze each opportunity to determine its potential for life enrichment. This step also involves detailing and documenting the desired outcomes.

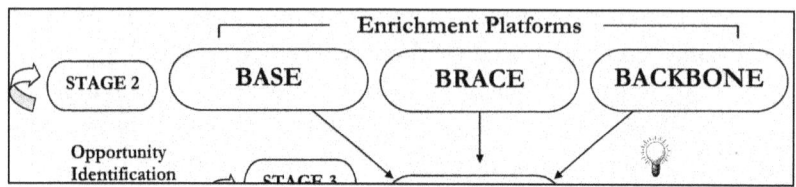

Figure 15-5 - Opportunity Identification

The components used to perform this step are contained in *Step-One* of the TWO-STEP Opportunity Identification Methodology. Figure 15-6 details the activity associated with opportunity identification.

Prior to this Stage, the results of the Framing Query have been used to identify the Enrichment Platform that is required to launch the Opportunity Identification Stage [See Figure 15-5]. From the Enrichment Platform you gain sufficient exposure to the representations and insights embodied within the *Platform Archetypes*.

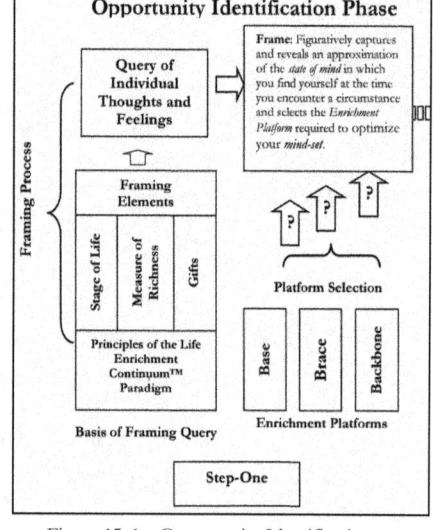

Figure 15-6 – Opportunity Identification

The objective is to ensure that the characterizations represented by the Framing Elements all have a "top-of-mind" position in your theater of thought as you establish your initial perception of the event.

The output of the Opportunity Identification Stage is a list of circumstances, embedded opportunities and desired outcomes associated with the event.

III. THE EXAMINATION AND PRIORITIZATION STAGE

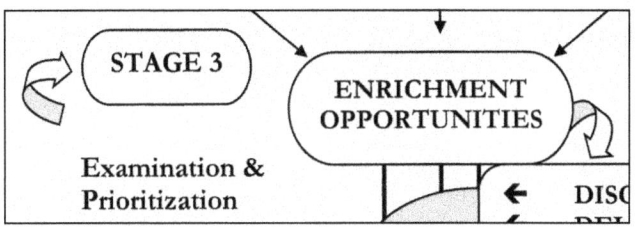

Figure 15-7 - Examination and Prioritization

The **Examination and Prioritization Stage** is the third step in the *Life Enrichment Model*™. In this stage the goal is to take the list of circumstances and associated opportunities generated within the Opportunity Identification Stage and decide which opportunities have the highest probability to enrich your life. The selected opportunities must also be within your reach and your ability to realize them at this time.

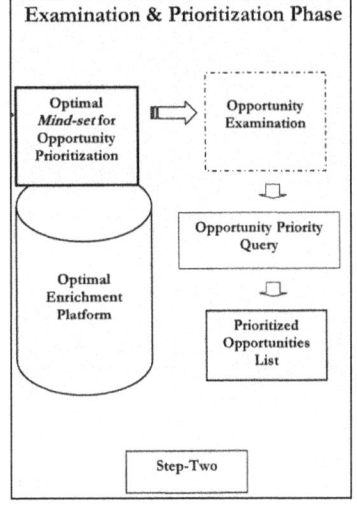

Figure 15-8 - TWO-STEP Methodology

The modeling components used to perform this step of the process is *Step-Two* of the Two-Step Opportunity Identification Methodology and a stimulating set of questions developed to focus your thoughts during opportunity prioritization, called the *Priority Query*. Figure 15-8 details the activity associated with the Opportunity Identification Phase. The *Priority Query* in presented in Figure 15-9.

The actual prioritization is determined by your responses to the *Priority Query*. The Examination and Prioritization Stage's output is a list of *actionable opportunities* which are believed to have the potential to shape a more positive outcome to the event at hand.

This set of circumstances and *actionable opportunities* becomes the focus of the last two stages of the model, **Enrichment Examination** and **Action Execution.**

> **Opportunity Priority Query**
>
> 1. *Do I have the physical, psychological & intellectual strength and stamina to take on what is required to move this situation, from where it is today, to where I envision it has to be, in order to obtain the value & richness I perceive it will add to my life, when fully realized?*
>
> 2. *Do I have or can I acquire the level of resources [financial, moral & spiritual] required to seize the opportunity?*
>
> 3. *If I decide to do nothing, am I ready to accept and live with the consequences that may arise as a result of this circumstance?*

Figure 15-9 - Opportunity Priority Query

IV. THE ENRICHMENT EXAMINATION STAGE
(Modal Exploration)

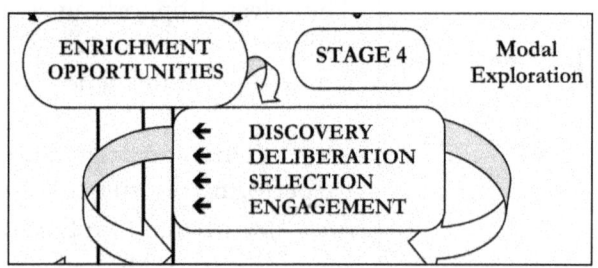

Figure 15-10 - The Modal Exploration Stage

The **Enrichment Examination Stage** is the fourth step in the *Life Enrichment Model*™. In this stage the goal is to sequentially and systematically examine more intensely each set of circumstances and *actionable opportunities* identified in the Examination and Prioritization Stage.

This intense examination uses a process called *Modal Exploration*. The Modal Exploration process is both thought provoking and methodical. With potential Enrichment Opportunities as its input, it utilizes a series of custom designed inquiries to lead you through a guided exploration of each circumstance. The output of a successful exploration is the completion of the actions as documented during the engagement mode.

Figure 15-11 summarizes the objectives and outcomes of each the four modes involved in the Modal Exploration Process.

The Enrichment Examination Stage culminates in the *Selection Mode*. In the Selection Mode you must decide to either *engage* in moving forward with the planning and execution of the tasks associated with *seizing* the enrichment opportunity or decide to not respond to the circumstance at hand in this fashion. A decision not to pursue the opportunity concludes the exploration.

Exploration Mode	Activity and Objectives
Discovery	• In the **Discovery Mode** the objective is to develop a concise summary and description of each circumstance surrounding the *event* or *situation* at hand. This activity is fueled by a thoughtful and thorough examination of all aspects of the situation. • This Mode also generates a concise set of statements that describe the opportunities available to you [at this time] in order to shape a more positive *outcome*, *result* and *future*, as a consequence of *the event* and *your response*.
Deliberation	• The **Deliberation Mode** involves the attainment of a detailed understanding of the opportunity and the documentation of *what will be required of you and others* in order to seize the opportunity.
Selection	• In the **Selection Mode** you must make a decision to either *pursue the opportunity* or to *respond to the circumstance* with another approach. • A decision NOT to pursue this *particular* opportunity concludes this exploration.
Engagement	• In the **Engagement Mode** you will develop and execute the *action plan* required to seize the opportunity. This mode also contains the follow-up activity required to determine the actual outcome and its impact on your life's richness.

Figure 15-11 - Modal Exploration

V. THE ACTION EXECUTION STAGE

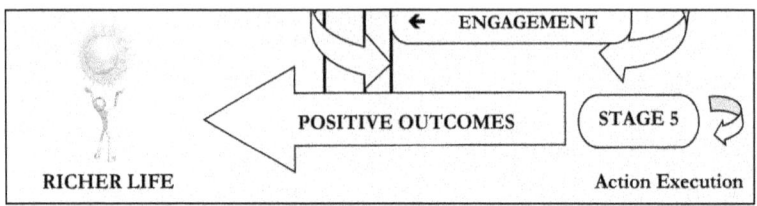

Figure 15-12 - The Action Execution Stage

The **Action Execution Stage** is the final step in the *Life Enrichment Model*™. This stage supports the execution of the actions developed and planned as a part of the Engagement Mode within the Modal Exploration process.

PART III

OPPORTUNITIES REVEALED:
PERSONAL NARRATIVES

The following narratives are formatted to correspond with the *five stages* associated with the Life Enrichment Model. In addition to being fortified and encouraged by the candid and detailed stories, you should view them as examples of the degree of detail you are seeking as the output (and insight) from each of the stages as you apply the Life Enrichment Model™ to a major circumstance in your life.

"We construct a narrative for ourselves, and that's the thread that we follow from one day to the next. People who disintegrate as personalities are the ones who lose that thread." - **Paul Auster**

"Narrative is linear, but action has breadth and depth as well as height and is solid." - **Thomas Carlyle**

CHAPTER SIXTEEN

A NEW HOUSE FOR MOM AND DAD

MODAL EXPLORATION

Discovery

In the late 1980's, Earl's parents were in their late sixties. Starting in the mid-1970's they had developed a ritual of traveling to visit their children's homes. They would regularly travel between Arizona, Colorado, Nebraska, West Virginia, South Carolina and Florida for lengthy stays during hot summers and cold winters.

However, by 1989, there were few trips being made. They also appeared to be slowing down. They shared with us that they were not up to fighting the crowds at the airports anymore and wanted to sleep in their own bed.

Earl's parents visiting Phoenix in 1989.

After Mom barely survived a serious case of pneumonia during the winter of 1991, Earl and I both became extremely concerned about their health. We were as concerned about their ability to properly maintain their health in the Cobb family's house located in the small

Mid-Georgia town of Vienna. Vienna is located about 140 miles due south of Atlanta, just off of Interstate I-75. Similar to most small towns in the South, it did not have many local services and reached its maximum population of around 4,000 back in the late 1950's.

Artice and Carrie Bell Cobb with Earl's youngest sister, Selma, in front of Cobb family home in 1955.

The Cobb family's home was built by Earl's dad during the evenings and on the weekends in the early 1950's. It was a small, four room house. This is where Earl was born and where his parents, Artice and Carrie Bell Cobb raised eight children.

Earl's father worked as a local painter, barber and handyman. He was also born in the Vienna area and only had the opportunity to obtain a fourth grade education. Earl's mom, affectionately called Carrie Bell, had a seventh grade education and was a stay-at-home mother. The only exception was that in order to make ends meet, she would occasionally take on an odd job cleaning other's homes and regularly performed seasonal work in the cotton fields during the summers. There never was much money. But, the home was always filled with love and wonderful memories. However, the house itself did not have central air or heat and was not suitable, in our minds, for our aging parents. The old home was also void of the space and amenities that we envisioned would be required as Earl and his seven siblings (and their children) would now need to regularly travel to Georgia to spend time with their aging parents in the coming years.

During this time, Earl was a group vice president with Motorola's Government and Systems Technology Group in Scottsdale, Arizona. He had just been promoted to head Motorola's world-wide military radio systems business unit. I was a vice president and senior manager with Norwest Bank in Phoenix. I was managing a large financial trust portfolio for the bank. Our only child, Brandi Reneè, was a teenager at the time. In other words, our personal financial situation was in fairly good shape. With our financial ability to address our parent's housing dilemma not being in question, we concluded the following:

Our Circumstance: If we do not improve the housing situation, it is possible that Mom would not survive another bout with pneumonia. The summer temperatures are presenting an increasing health threat to both Mom and Dad without adequate air conditioning. As they continue to age, they will not be able to safely light the old gas stove in the living room used to heat the entire house in the winter months. Furthermore, it is not certain that we will continue to have the financial fortunes and wherewithal to seriously address the dilemma that the lack of adequate housing would continue to present.

Our Opportunity: If it is our desire to improve Mom and Dad's housing situation, then now is the time to adequately respond to this circumstance. We could wait and react to the next bout of pneumonia or the next health issue. But, we both know that ignoring the root cause of the problem and simply reacting to the symptoms would not address our real concerns. By responding now, in a proactive and thoughtful manner, we would take advantage of our ability to finance the improvements as well as maximize the amount of quality time we would have to spend with them in the future.

Deliberation

While deliberating on what we could do and how, we concluded that we needed to at least do the following prior to making a final "selection'" regarding the situation at hand.

- We must agree among ourselves whether we truly wanted to commit a portion of our income to build and maintain a new house in Georgia.

    It did not take us long to come to the conclusion that the investment would not only be good for Mom and Dad but would also provide a potential tax write-off against future income. In addition, it would eliminate the need for us and others to reserve hotel rooms during our visits to Vienna.

- We had to determine how to convince Earl's parents to allow us to build the house for them. Mrs. Carrie Bell had previously stated many times that she did not want any of her children spending money on them. She was adamant about not wanting to hear her children "fussing" over who did what for them.

We were able to convince Earl's parents by assuring them that we "both" felt strongly about building the new house. We also were able to convince them that it would not be a burden on us since we both were gainfully employed and had promising careers. We promised that we would address any family issues upfront by speaking with all of Earl's sisters and brothers to get their approval and support.

- We had to actually obtain Earl's siblings approval and support for the idea.

We started with Earl's oldest sister Laura. Her long-time husband, Alex, had died of prostate cancer a few years earlier. She expressed the possibility of her being in a position to relocate back to Georgia in the near future. She marveled at the idea of having a new house in Vienna. The improved living conditions would aid in her efforts to be able to care for Mom and Dad at home in their later years. Earl's conversations with Doris, Artice Jr., Andrew, Gloria, Selma and Alfonso also were extremely positive. They all were in varying stages of raising families and were not in the position themselves to take an equity stake in the project. However, they all indicated that they would help wherever they could.

- Then, we had to develop a plan for getting the job done while both of us were at the peak of our careers and living 2000 miles from the construction site.

This was most challenging. We agreed that it was important to select a good local construction contractor that we could trust. We both also felt that is was important that we share the undertaking with our respective managers at work so that they would understand why we might have to take a number of three-day weekends over the next few months to fly down to the work site for periodic inspections.

Selection

After reviewing the financial arrangements, investigating the possibility of obtaining a local building contractor to perform the work and completing all discussions with Earl's parents & siblings, we selected a response to this circumstance. We decided to move forward with a project to build Mom and Dad a new house in Georgia. We named the undertaking, *Project Love*.

Our response was based on our belief that a new house was what was needed based the condition at hand. In addition, we believed that its utility would enrich the lives of our entire family. A new Cobb home would not only become a place for the Cobb family and friends to frequently gather and maintain loving relationships but would also provide a more comfortable and safer place for Mom and Dad to live. Moreover, it could possibly extend the amount of time we would have to enjoy them.

Engagement

The new house being constructed on original home site.

Once we had decided to move forward with the project, we knew that a focused engagement effort was critical. Just as important was the need for us to take action quickly to establish some momentum. We developed a plan to build the new home on the same lot where the existing home was located. This would allow Mom and Dad to remain in their old house while the new house was being constructed. This arrangement was essential. It was also a determining factor to getting Mom and Dad to agree with the new home construction.

Earl finalized Mom and Dad's approval to proceed with the new home construction by getting them to deed the land over to us. We worked with a local attorney to make sure the property lines were surveyed and accurately recorded in the Dooly County records. The attorney had known Artice and Carrie Bell for years. His initial concern was that we might not live up to this undertaking and leave Mom and Dad out in the cold. But, once he was briefed on the plans and sensed our level of commitment, his concerns quickly subsided. The deed transfer was necessary to enable the mortgage financing. It also ensured that the value of the property improvement would not impact Mom and Dad's Social Security and Medicare --- their only source of retirement income and medical coverage.

We then established a banking relationship with the local bank in Vienna and opened a joint checking account with Mom and Dad. The account would initially be used to retain the funds required for landscaping expenses and to pay Mortgage closing costs. The account would be replenished on a monthly basis to provide funds to cover property taxes and home maintenance expenses.

Over the following months, we began to execute a long list of activities which included the following:

- We identified and hired a reputable, local building contractor.

    This was not an easy chore. We eventually had to travel to Dublin, a Georgia town about 80 miles from Vienna, to find a contractor we felt comfortable with and could trust to build the new family home.

- We developed the home construction plans and obtained the zoning and building permits.

    We shared all of the home plans with Earl's parents as they were being drafted. Mom and Dad both were involved in making final decisions on kitchen design, flooring, closets and light fixtures. They really enjoyed being involved in the decision making process. It was great to see the renewed energy in both Mom and Dad. It appeared that just the idea of getting a new house had already began to add years onto their lives.

- We obtained local financing for a new home mortgage.

- We managed the three month construction project while living in Arizona, some 2,000 miles from the construction site.

- We performed periodic construction inspections and eventually a final walk through prior to accepting the finished product.

- We developed a plan, along with Earl's sisters and brothers, to move Mom and Dad into their new home.

The home site prior to removing the old house.

However, one item we had to carefully address was how to remove the old house from the site. We all knew that this would be an emotional transition for Mom and Dad. The old house was more than a house. It was the place that Dad had built with his own hands. It was the place where Mom and Dad had raised their family together and where they had lived for over 40 years.

As it turned out, it was Mrs. Carrie who became aware of a federal housing program that eventually would agree to accept and pay to move the old house. I recall Mom calling Earl in his office at Motorola one afternoon. Earl said that she seem so excited. She could not wait to share that she had identified a method by wish she would save us the cost of moving the old house. More importantly, she was ecstatic that the plan would not require that the old house be demolished.

Outcomes

Construction of the new house and the new Cobb home was completed in January 1993. With the help of their daughters, Mom and Dad moved into the new home later that month.

It is a 1,800 sq. ft., four bedroom, ranch-style house with central air conditioning and heating. The master bedroom is equipped with bathroom hand rails and other fixtures that Mom and Dad would need as they became less mobile. All three guest bedrooms are on the south end of the house. This was to accommodate the visiting family members and to provide Mom and Dad their needed privacy. The backyard features a custom deck built around a huge pecan tree that had been on the family lot for nearly 60 years.

Artice and Carrie Bell Cobb in Front of Their New House in Vienna.

We were able to donate the old house to the Federal Housing program. The program paid to move the old house to a new home site. The program remodeled the house, added a small porch and made it available to a low income family in the local area.

The old house is now located just nine miles away from the original home site. Mom was very pleased to see the old house still providing a home for another happy family. Over the next two decades, the new Cobb home would host many family re-unions and celebrations --- including Mom and Dad's 71st wedding Anniversary.

The Cobbs new home.

Mrs. Carrie Bell was a great cook and she thoroughly enjoyed her new kitchen. Everyone in Vienna were sure to attend the Saint Mark Baptist Church's "Big Meetings" (the local vernacular for major church events such as anniversaries) to get their hands on Mom's pineapple layer cakes and pecan pies. She lived to see her 87th birthday before peacefully being called to her heavenly home on June 29, 2009 after a lengthy bout with Alzheimer's disease.

Earl's Dad, now age 93, and his oldest sister, Laura, are presently living in the "new" house. The house is still the Cobb family's home and the family gathering place for special occasions.

Most of the Cobb Family together during the 1993 family reunion.

Thoughts Regarding Our Exploration

The time we spent together working on *Project Love* in the early 1990's contributed to strengthening our marriage and enriching our life. Our confidence in our career success and our desire to maintain, leverage and strengthen family relationships were significant factors in guiding our mind-set during this period of our life.

Being comfortable with who we were as individuals and as a couple, allowed us to emotionally recognize and accept the challenges associated with shaping the outcome of this circumstance such that we could seize the enrichment opportunities.

A deeper understanding of our decision making tendencies and what we valued in personal relationships during this time in our life allowed us to come to the conclusion that the circumstance we faced did not only encompass the well-being of Earl's parents. It also encompassed the love we had for each other, our mutual need for family closeness and the personal benefit we both gain from sharing our financial gifts with family and friends. In addition, and certainly without prior intent, by initiating and following through with *Project Love*, we inched closer to shaping a part of the legacy we would leave with generations of family members to come.

Being aware of the importance of the internal and external factors in our life and having the wherewithal to make a decision that would continue to enrich our life for decades into the future generated a different view of our life together. We began to see life, not simply as a collection of random events but as a continuum of opportunity for growth and life enrichment.

CHAPTER SEVENTEEN

STAYING IN OUR DAUGHTER'S LIFE

MODAL EXPLORATION

Discovery

Earl and Charlotte relax in their Tempe, Arizona home with Brandi, Age 5, in 1982.

On a warm May morning in 1987 Charlotte and I were having a long discussion while enjoying a cup of Starbuck's coffee in the kitchen of our home in Mill Creek, Washington. The topic centered on whether or not we should relocate back to the Phoenix area. I had just received an offer to return to Motorola as a senior program manager. I had already tentatively accepted the offer extended to me by the division general manager and long-time mentor. However, knowing my overall situation at the time, he gave me a week or so to make the final decision.

We had moved to the Seattle area in July of 1986. Charlotte had completed her MBA at Arizona State University. Shortly after graduation she was offered the opportunity to become a stockbroker with a well-known investment firm. She had been heavily recruited by the company. However, we had to relocate to accept a position in their Seattle office. We both agreed that it was an excellent opportunity for her and one that we should take full advantage.

Conversely, leaving the Phoenix area required that I leave my management position and the ten years I had invested in my career with Motorola. I was fortunate and quickly landed an opportunity to become the Manager of Program Management with the Power Conversion Division of ELDEC, a mid-market company located in Mill Creek, a Seattle suburb.

Brandi and Charlotte enjoy a playful moment in 1981.

Prior to deciding to leave Phoenix in 1986, I had reached an agreement with my ex-wife, Angela, regarding how we were to maintain joint custody of our daughter, Brandi Renee. Brandi was turning nine later that year and was eager to move into her third year of school. The agreement would allow Charlotte and me to enroll Brandi in a Seattle school that fall.

Angela and I had agreed on a shared custody arrangement as a part of our divorce decree in 1981. The agreement allowed Brandi to spend six months of the year with each parent. We had successfully maintained an amiable relationship regarding our daughter and her well-being since our initial separation in 1979. Angela and I both agreed that I was in a better station in life, at the time, to provide for the education of our daughter.

Brandi was four years old when Charlotte and I were married in 1982. She was in our wedding and had always been a part of our family. Shortly after we settled in Seattle in July 1986, we began discussing with Angela the logistics around Brandi's move to Seattle.

However, in September of 1986, Angela surprisingly shared with us that she had changed her mind. She was planning to keep our daughter in Phoenix.

Charlotte and I both were around thirty years old at the time. We were quite mature for our age and were comfortable with our personal and professional lives. Yet, Angela's decision produced an unexpected and emotionally significant event in our life. Quite frankly, it spun the first jointly shared set of potentially life altering circumstances we had experienced since we were married. We quickly realized that the choice of our initial response to the most pressing circumstance was quite binary. We could either remain in Seattle, a place we had really come to love and to call our new home *without* our daughter or return to Phoenix and forge a means to stay in our daughter's life during her most formative years.

Charlotte hugs Brandi at her wedding in 1982. Brandi was the ring bearer.

During our initial evaluation of our dilemma, we discovered several circumstances that had to be addressed as well as potential opportunities to enrich our lives. Among the circumstances was the need to orchestrate another major move in less than a couple of years and the requirement to navigate the uncertainty of another career change for both of us. Of the potential opportunities, the one that stood out as most promising was the possible lifelong benefits that could be gained from being in a position to have a positive influence on our daughter and her life. Being closer to her geographically would mean being available to provide the moral, spiritual and additional financial support she would need on a consistent basis. After much thought and discussion, we concluded the following:

Our Circumstance: It would be easier for us to *simply accept* this unilateral change in plan as the response to our circumstance.

However, we knew that with this response, *the circumstance* itself would continue to dictate how and when we would be involved in our daughter's life. In addition, we would have to live the rest of our life not knowing how things might have been different if we had placed ourselves in a position to be closer to our daughter and in her life on a daily basis. On the contrary, we knew that we could not simply just move back to Phoenix. We must also be willing and capable of taking whatever actions that would be necessary to remain in our daughter's life in a meaningful way.

Our Opportunity: As stated above, being closer to Brandi geographically would mean being available to provide what she would need on a consistent basis. On the other hand, we both understood that there was no guarantee that being physically closer to our daughter would result in her meeting our expectations or ensure that her life would be one of achievement. There was also no way of knowing what she would add to or take away from our life. Nonetheless, we believed that our lives would be enriched by the opportunity to have a constructive and engaging place in our daughter's life. We also felt strongly that we needed to cultivate a relationship with Brandi that would be significant and long lasting.

Deliberation

During our deliberation, we compiled a list of things we needed to more closely examine and thoroughly understand. The list of items focused around Angela's decision to keep Brandi in Phoenix and how we would manage a successful relocation back to Phoenix. We knew that we had to carefully construct a transition that would support our ultimate objective.

Our final list included the following:

- We had to determine if there was the possibility that Angela would eventually have a change of mind (and heart) and move forward with what we believed was the original agreement of allowing Brandi to be enrolled in the Seattle school system.

> *In subsequent discussions with Angela, I learned that she was steadfast in her decision not to honor her earlier agreement. I also sensed that her decision was slanted more toward the child support payments versus a genuine concern with Brandi's education. Per the divorce decree, Angela would not receive the several hundred dollars of monthly child support payments during the time Brandi was not staying with her.*

- We had to investigate the possibility of Charlotte not having to resign her position with Dean Witter Reynolds by transferring to another position within the company in the Phoenix area.

> *After several weeks of pursuing this possibility, Charlotte finally received her answer regarding the transfer request. Although the idea was intriguing and supported by her immediate supervisor, there were no immediate transfer opportunities in Phoenix at that time. This unearthed another circumstance that we would have to address. Charlotte would now have to seek a new position with another financial services company upon our return to Phoenix.*

Brandi dressed in school uniform at age six.

- I needed to negotiate a final offer with Motorola that would help defray the moving and relocation expenses. We anticipated that we would have to quickly get settled back in Phoenix in order to immediately initiate a new job search for Charlotte. We also needed to initiate our efforts to get our daughter enrolled in a good school close to our new home that fall.

> *I was able to present a good case as to the value I would bring to Motorola and the program management position. My relationship with Motorola management, the timing and the need to fill the position with experience, resulted in me obtaining an excellent relocation package, including a cash bonus. The generous relocation*

> *package would support our need to complete a timely transition and financially support our efforts to stay in our daughter's life.*

- We had to construct a plan. The plan would need to be one that we were capable and willing to execute. We knew that, at a minimum, we would have to maintain the six-month custody arrangement established in the 1981 divorce decree. However, we felt that due to the unexpected adversarial relationship that was developing between us and Brandi's mother, it may be necessary to pursue an extended custody arrangement in order to provide the environment that our daughter would need to truly benefit from our return.

> *We would have to prepare ourselves both financially and emotionally to make sure that we were in a position to seize this opportunity. It would be important that we were also in a position to shape a positive outcome to this unexpected event for our daughter as well as ourselves. We both were well aware that this ordeal would test the strength of our marriage and our resolve.*

Selection

Following what seemed to us to be a thorough and successful period of deliberation, I accepted Motorola's offer to return to Phoenix. We both resigned our positions with two wonderful companies and prepared ourselves for our mission to stay in our daughter's life.

We selected a course of action which, in our minds, provided us a reasonable chance to seize the opportunity at hand. The deliberate response we selected to address the circumstances surrounding this major event in our life was developed by evaluating a multitude of factors. However, both of us had agreed that the primary reason to make another move at this time was to put ourselves in the best position to cultivate a relationship with our daughter that would be significant and long lasting. We also wanted to never to be in the position of wondering *what might have been different* in all of our lives if we had not made a move at this time. We coined this episode in our life, *Project Hope*.

Engagement

We completed our return to the Phoenix area in July of 1987. I immediately started my new position with Motorola's Government and Systems Technology Group in Scottsdale.

Charlotte quickly initiated her search for a new job. Based on the downturn in the stock market and the brokerage business in 1987, she decided to pursue a position in banking. To our good fortune, Charlotte secured a position with Citibank Arizona (which subsequently became Norwest Bank and then Wells Fargo Bank). She started as an institutional trust portfolio manager.

Brandi following family vacation to Hawaii to celebrate her 16th Birthday.

Over the next ten years, we would add to and build upon proactive and reactive episodes associated with *Project Hope*. We would also witness an unexpected and significant growth in our personal strength, our professional achievements and our financial worth --- all as an offshoot of our decision to return to Phoenix and to stay in our daughter's life.

Some of the most memorable activities and outcomes associated with our undertaking to stay in our daughter's life during her formative years included the following:

- Purchasing a new home in north Scottsdale and getting Brandi enrolled in the fourth grade in the Scottsdale Unified School System.

- Hiring an attorney to represent us in a renewed child custody battle spurred on by Brandi's mother's decision and legal action to gain full custody.

- Securing the services of a clinical psychologist to aid in determining the family environment that would best support both the psychological and educational development of our daughter.

- Reaching an agreement which provided us with legal custody of our daughter for nine months of the year along with Brandi spending the summers with her mother. We agreed to pay Angela the monthly child support even during the months that Brandi lived with us.

- Enrolling Brandi in a new middle school in Scottsdale and providing Brandi with tutorial services to support and strengthen her math and science skills.

- Enrolling Brandi in a Scottsdale Boys and Girls Clubs after school program. Brandi also worked as a volunteer and won an outstanding achievement award.

- Taking a family trip during school break to Hawaii to celebrate Brandi's 16th birthday.

- Enrolling Brandi in High School in Scottsdale and providing support of her interest in theater.

- Planning and taking trips with Brandi to several colleges and universities, including Tennessee State, Spelman and Clark-Atlanta, to explore potential interest.

- Responding to challenges of Brandi's adolescence and her rejection of our values and accomplishment-oriented lifestyle.

- Eventually agreeing to Brandi's constant request to move back in with her mother during her junior year in high school and withdrawing from a quality Scottsdale School system.

Outcomes

As we mentioned earlier, going into *Project Hope,* Charlotte and I both were well aware that the ordeal would most likely test the strength of our marriage and our resolve.

In hindsight, our analysis of the actual outcomes and subsequent events associated with *Project Hope* reminded us of a quote attributed to Sasha Azevedo, an American actress, athlete and model. She was once asked about how she faces life's challenges. She responded with the following:

"I do believe that when we face challenges in life that are far beyond our own power, it's an opportunity to build on our faith, inner strength, and courage. I've learned that how we face challenges plays a big role in the outcome of them."

We believe that we faced the challenges associated with our sincere efforts to cultivate a significant and long lasting relationship with our daughter with *faith, strength* and *courage*. We also took into the undertaking realistic expectations and a commitment to effectively manage, in parallel, all of the other aspects of our life.

During the same period of our life which was consumed by *Project Hope*, our personal, professional and community life flourished as a result of us encountering and successfully responding to new events and circumstances.

Earl (standing far left) was one of the seven African-American Vice Presidents in all of Motorola, Inc. in 1995.

Charlotte survived multiple bank mergers and became a vice president with Norwest Bank where she headed a large corporate trust portfolio. I received several promotions within Motorola and assumed executive responsibilities for large business activities. In 1993, I became a group vice president, traveled extensively internationally and later headed Motorola's world-wide military radio systems business.

Charlotte's Parents, Alberta and Julius Grant - Following their move to Colorado Springs.

Charlotte and I both were on multiple Boards of Phoenix area civic and community organizations. We finally were able to spend some quality time with Charlotte's parents who had moved from their family home in Alaska to their retirement home in Colorado Springs. We even took on another Project and built my parents a new house down in middle Georgia.

Even with all of the other demands placed on us we still dedicated quality time and made a concentrated effort to have an engaging relationship with our daughter.

However, as Brandi struggled with adolescence, we struggled with penetrating a *mental wall* that Brandi seemed to have established between her and us. It appeared then, as it does now, that this *wall* is constructed to separate, in her mind, the two fundamentally different lifestyles tugging for her affection.

As a result, the *Project Hope* engagement period turned out to be one of the *most rewarding*, yet one of the *most disappointing* decades of our life together.

Thoughts Regarding Our Exploration

Nonetheless, as we reflect back on our efforts to not only stay in our daughter's life but to become an engaging and influential force, we can see how we succeeded on several fronts.

We will never have to wonder *what might have been different* in all of our lives if we had *not* decided, in 1987, to relocate back to Phoenix. We were there, we gave it our best and we, in hindsight, became better individuals and a closer couple as a result of *responding* versus simply *reacting* to this life altering circumstance.

As we recall, our initial thoughts were to *react* to Angela's decision by shutting down and just saying *"the heck with it"*. We, for a brief moment, might have thought that our life would have been better during that time if all we had to do was send a check every month and pay for a plane ticket to visit with Brandi during the holidays and school breaks. However, we were aware that it was not the major events in our life that had necessarily determined our life's outcomes. We knew that, to the contrary, many outcomes were dependent upon how well we responded to the resulting circumstances. Our response to this circumstance required us to take the time, dedicate the resources and use our natural gifts to shape the best outcome.

Brandi, age 21, during a visit to our Ohio home in 1998.

Because we believed that life was more than simply a collection of random events, we allowed the other facets in our life [i.e. careers, relationships, education, goals, etc.] to continue to take their course as we still maintained focus on our daughter and the relationship we believed would enrich all three of our lives.

Even with all of the *twists and turns* taken during *Project Hope*, we still love and we are proud of our daughter.

We are also just as proud of the three beautiful and vastly different grandchildren she has brought into this world and into our life. We know that it was our *responses* to a number of difficult circumstances during *Project Hope* that laid the path for all six of us to be in a position to enjoy each other's earthly presence.

Just as we have hope for a richer life for our grandchildren, we also continue to be in a hopeful relationship with our daughter.

We all should be reminded from time to time of the words of George Eliott, *"It is never too late to be what you might have been"*.

CHAPTER EIGHTEEN

BECOMING A FRANCHISE OWNER

MODAL EXPLORATION

Discovery

In September of 1999, Charlotte and I had just returned from an eight day Caribbean cruise. We were in the process of relocating from our home in Butler Township, just North of Dayton, Ohio, to a new home we were in the process of purchasing in an area known as Lake Norman, North Carolina. Lake Norman was a new and growing suburb about 15 miles north of Charlotte NC.

Charlotte and Earl on cruise ship in 1999.

The inviting Lake Norman community had evolved over a 60 year period with homes eventually peppering a 450 mile man-made lake which was master planned as a part of a Duke Energy nuclear power plant.

The relocation was the result of my corporate vice president position with the Reynolds and Reynolds Company being eliminated following the sale of the company's Healthcare Systems Division. We made the decision not to remain in the Dayton area in the summer of 1999.

Based on an ongoing economic recession and the challenges in the job market, we were leaning toward pursuing an entrepreneurial lifestyle. We had visited a close friend, Clement Ashford, in Charlotte, North Carolina several months earlier. We immediately fell in love with Lake Norman. We were fortunate to find a beautiful home in a quiet cove known as Sterling Point just off of Interstate 77 and Highway 77. The 3,000 sq. ft. ranch style home was on the lake and included a private boat slip located only a short distance from our back yard. We would later purchase a 24-foot Harris Kayot pontoon cruiser and enjoy entertaining friends with sight-seeing tours of the vast lake and tranquil environment. The new house and the freshness of the Charlotte, NC region appeared to be just perfect for the next phase of our life.

The Cobb's Lake Norman home in 1999.

Earl, Charlotte and friend Marty onboard the Cobb's pontoon cruiser named "MJ".

As a part of our move to Dayton in 1997, Charlotte had decided to not seek new employment and to take a sabbatical to pursue a second post graduate degree. In 1999, Charlotte completed the course work and began work on her dissertation. She would soon receive a well-earned professional Doctorate Degree in Nutrition Counseling from LaSalle University.

We actually began our discussions regarding Charlotte's return to the workforce when we first arrived in Dayton. A nutrition-based retail business and the category of customers it would attract would complement the nutritional consulting and coaching practice she had planned to launch after graduation. Following the Reynolds and Reynolds experience and the need now to move quickly toward new sources of income, we began to more seriously consider an investment in a national retail franchise to make this idea a reality.

After returning from vacation in mid-September, we began to more aggressively research the nutrition products industry. We were most interested in identifying the best franchising opportunities. Through her research, Charlotte determined that the top rated company, General Nutrition Centers or GNC, was offering new franchises in the United States and that a Charlotte, NC location was a possibility. GNC appeared to have a unique business model. It had developed both company-owned and franchised outlets in comparable numbers. We decided to pursue the idea of becoming GNC owner/operators. After completing the necessary applications and other documents we continued to further investigate the company and its franchise format. Several weeks into the process, we learned that we had been pre-qualified as a potential franchisee.

Thus, by December 1999, it was appearing as if the "stars were lining up" for us to move to Charlotte, NC and purchase a GNC franchise as our first entry into a new entrepreneurial lifestyle. We were both excited about the idea. We could afford the franchise fee and investment required. We liked the Charlotte, NC market and the franchisor seemed to be offering a proven and successful business format.

However, we had to factor into our decision the fact that even though I had obtained an excellent severance package from Reynolds and Reynolds, becoming entrepreneurs at this stage in life (we were both in our mid-forties) may not support the corporate life style of which we had become accustomed.

Our Circumstance: After 25 years, we found ourselves in a dilemma, where due to corporate downsizing neither of us was employed. Yet, we had become accustomed to a corporate lifestyle and income level. The most pressing circumstance spun by this potential life altering event was the need to replace our income source --- preferably with the opportunity that matched our current experience and aspirations.

We needed to decide whether to primarily focus on finding new corporate jobs, in a challenging employment environment of the late 1990's or pursue other alternatives. Of course, the most likely option at this stage of life would be to leverage our extensive business training and experience in some entrepreneurial capacity.

Our Opportunity: To take advantage of the wealth we had accumulated and the timing of this unexpected transition, we should respond to our genuine desire to enter the world of entrepreneurship and possible financial independence. Even though we would risk not being able to replace our previous income levels, we both valued and were passionate about the possibility of utilizing our business development skills and potentially establishing a successful business.

We envisioned the initial business success leading to the establishment of a viable, long term family-owned enterprise. We often talked about establishing such an enterprise which would be available for our daughter, grandchildren, nieces and nephews to leverage as a starting point and possible employment fallback as they worked to carve out the next generation of livelihoods for themselves and their families.

Deliberation

During our deliberation, we thought it would be prudent to more closely analyze both the circumstance in which we found ourselves and the "pros and cons" associated with moving too quickly into starting our own business. Consequently, we compiled two separate lists. Each list outlined what we needed to consider more thoroughly prior to selecting a response to the circumstance at hand.

Regarding the circumstance, we outlined the two key areas we felt we should more thoroughly explore.

- We should develop a household budget to determine how long we could sustain ourselves at the current lifestyle until we needed to supplement our monthly cash flow with new income.

    Since we had always maintained a monthly household budget and were fortunate to have been in a position for a number of years to not have to accumulate any major credit card or consumer debt, we were able to rather quickly determine that, by prudently stretching the monthly severance payments, we could sustain ourselves for 12 to 18 months.

- We should make an assessment of whether or not one or both of us should pursue a new corporate position and the potential negative impact on future corporate opportunities, for either or both of us, if we were out of the corporate work force for a substantial period of time.

   With Charlotte having left the corporate workforce in 1997 when we moved from Scottsdale to Dayton, she was already a couple of years removed from her banking career and the corporate work force. The probability for her returning anywhere similar to the level and pay grade that she vacated in a banking environment that was rapidly consolidating seemed remote. Furthermore, it would be her knowledge of nutrition and retail that would be needed to strategically plan the start-up of a new GNC franchise.

   Since I was part of a group of senior managers who had been displaced and were viewed as "casualties of the dot-com shake out" during the national recession of the late 1990's, I felt that I should have the opportunity to get back into a comparable position within 6 to 8 months.

   However, the technical management position for which I would be best suited most likely would not be found in the Charlotte, NC region. Based on the fact that it would take months before we would open a new GNC franchise in North Carolina and that it would be Charlotte who would oversee most of the day-to-day operation, it made sense for me to leverage my multi-industry background and pursue a new corporate position as soon as possible.

   My successful tenures with some well-respected companies like Motorola and Reynolds and Reynolds should serve me well. On the other hand, if I am out of the executive pace for too long, it would become increasingly difficult to land a comparable position without some serious re-invention.

In terms of the "pros and cons" associated with moving too quickly into starting our own business, we compiled the following list of areas that we felt required further consideration:

- We should perform a significant amount of due diligence to ensure the viability of General Nutrition Center franchises and the quality of GNC's training and support for new franchisees.

  We actually began our due diligence of GNC several months prior to deciding to move to Charlotte. At the time, GNC was one of the largest and most popular franchisors in the world. The company had opened over 4,000 stores in the United States and over 1,200 franchise operations in 52 international markets. For nearly 75 years, GNC had been building a global reputation as the largest specialty retailer of nutritional products. We spoke with several current franchise owner/operators regarding their overall experience with the company, the products, the marketing strategies and the support they obtained from the corporate office. We also inquired about their actual financial performance vs. their initial expectations. The vast majority of the owner/operators we spoke with were quite pleased with their decision to become a GNC franchisee.

- We should understand the level of investment required and what to expect in terms of net income and profitability.

  We visited the GNC corporate office in Pittsburg, Pennsylvania. We spent a full day gaining visibility into their franchise system and discussing historical performance of new stores. For a total investment of approximately $125,000 to $200,000, including about $80,000 of capital equipment, we could expect to retain 7 to 10% profit on an average of $600,000 of sales revenue per store. It became obvious that in order to generate a net income of over $100,000, we would have to invest in multiple stores over time.

- We should perform our own analysis of the Charlotte, NC market to understand how well existing stores were performing and the available new store locations.

    Based on a collection of data provided by GNC and our own visits to the major locations in the greater Charlotte area, we found the Charlotte, NC market to be slightly above average. Knowing that past performance is no guarantee of future performance, we still felt comfortable with the growing Charlotte region and the new store sites that were available. Our first choice was a site designed with a new store format that GNC had recently developed. The new "store-in-store" format included smaller 800 to 1,000 sq. ft. stores located inside large, upscale grocery retailers. Most of the grocery stores also included bank locations. Even though the average revenue was smaller in stores with this format, the safety of not being located in a strip mall and the convenience of being able to make cash deposits without leaving the location were all attractive features --- especially with Charlotte planning to spend quite a bit of time in the store and managing the operations.

Selection

After carefully weighing all of our options, we selected a two pronged response to this circumstance. We would move forward with purchasing our first GNC franchise with Charlotte initially operating it solo. In addition, I would aggressively search for a new corporate position. Thus, we dubbed this journey, *Project 2-Source*

With the financial wherewithal to give ourselves the time needed to fully pursue both paths, we began by developing a detailed business plan for the GNC business and utilizing an executive search consultant provided by Reynolds and Reynolds.

Engagement

The executive search portion of the response to our most pressing circumstance was fairly straight forward. With the assistance of a New York based consultant, provided as a part of my severance package, an effective search could be executed smoothly. The process included the usual: the development of an updated resume, the sharpening of focus on the industries/companies to be pursued, daily networking with colleagues and waiting for the right opportunity to surface. We knew that finding a new corporate position in a challenging employment economy would take time. Based on the approach we were taking as a response to our circumstance, this would provide the opportunity for me to remain in North Carolina, at least initially, as we tackled the new challenge of establishing a new business in a new city.

As planned, Charlotte took the lead in our effort to become a franchise owner and operator. Over the next four years we would start a business, grow a business and eventually close a business. The following are the most memorable events and significant milestones we encountered.

- Following nine months of preparatory tasks and activities, CobbCare GNC opened in December 2000. The GNC corporate office could not finalize the lease agreement with our first selection of location. Typically, it was GNC's real estate department which selected physical store sites well in advance of a store opening. Then, GNC would either open a company store on the site or sublease the space to a franchisee. After months of waiting, we agreed to purchase a company-owned store located about three miles north of our initial site selection. The store was one of the first outlets built inside a regional, high-end grocery store. The monthly sales revenue of the existing location was about half of where it should have been for this size store. Charlotte and her new

Dr. Grant-Cobb as she works in new GNC.

CobbCare GNC team would have to really work to get this location up to expectations.

> *The activities leading to the grand opening required a significant amount of planning. Charlotte worked with the various GNC contacts to make it all happen on time and within budget. The activities included: negotiating and signing of a franchise agreement which specified the new "store-in-store" format; hiring the initial staff; attending a two-week, mandatory training class at the GNC corporate headquarters; working with GNC real estate to identify and select store location; finalizing the design and layout of the store; agreeing to a build-out schedule and planning the grand opening; acquiring the necessary point of sale processing services; developing the first 90 day marketing and advertising plan; placing the first order for start-up product inventories; stocking of store; preparing signage for grand opening and distributing grand opening advertising.*

- By the spring of 2001, Charlotte had doubled the monthly sales revenue. She strategically integrated select third party products with the GNC standard products in support of diabetic and menopausal health. She attracted a loyal following of customers, including our pastor, his family and a large number of church members. She instituted a value shoppers program which rewarded frequent shoppers. She sponsored local "strong men" contests and significantly increased her sales of sports products. To her surprise, Charlotte was approached by the marketing department of the local university to participate in a program where students would develop competitive marketing plans based on her store location and product mix. The unique collaboration with the university provided some significant marketing and advertising insights.

Charlotte and friend Ginny during Grand Opening of General Nutrition Center.

- However, as the performance of the store continued to *soar*, CobbCare GNC's relationship with its landlord began to *sour*. The grocery store landlord refused to honor its agreement with GNC corporate to terminate the sale of certain nutritional items in their grocery store. During the holidays in 2002, the grocery store manager consistently placed grocery products in front of our store and refused to honor the terms of our lease agreement which prohibited such placement. We later learned the grocer was in the process of adding an in-store pharmacy and had targeted the space we were leasing to accommodate the addition.

- In the fall of 2003, after several attempts to get GNC corporate to enforce our lease agreement with the grocer, we had no choice other than to proceed with legal action. We quickly reached a settlement with GNC and the grocer. Based on our overall experience with the landlord and GNC corporate during the previous three years, we decided to accept a cash buyout versus opening CobbCare GNC at another Charlotte, NC location.

Outcomes

Our primary objective of establishing a new income source following my departure from Reynolds and Reynolds and our move to Charlotte, NC was accomplished on both fronts.

Charlotte and Earl in their GNC Store.

The CobbCare GNC business success proved that we had what it takes to truly be entrepreneurial and generate major income. During the three full years of operation, Charlotte grossed in the mid to high five figures in annual sales revenue. With the unfortunate settlement that led to the closing of CobbCare GNC, we recovered our initial investment and then some. In February of 2001, I accepted a position as COO with a venture-capital-backed IT start-up with a great salary and stock ownership. More importantly I earned the opportunity to lead the company as its CEO through the tail-end of the dot-com era.

By responding to a major circumstance in a manner which encompassed our aspirations as well as our immediate financial needs, we gained significantly more than another income source.

As we are reminded by the Chinese Proverb, *"Give a man a fish and you feed him for a day. Teach a man to fish and you feed him for a lifetime."*

Thoughts Regarding Our Exploration

Certainly by being prepared financially to *weather a storm* as significant as major income loss was of tremendous value to us. On the other hand, as we reflect back on this event in our life, it becomes obvious that just as important as having had financial reserves was our ability to recognize all of our gifts (natural and acquired) and how we could leverage them to shape positive outcomes to major circumstances.

We lived in the Charlotte, NC area for a total of six years. During this time, in addition to addressing the challenges associated with *Project 2-Source*, we found the time to build many long lasting friendships. We were pleasantly surprised with the genuineness and helpfulness of both the professional and personal relationships we established. We found all of our acquaintances to be good people with plenty of goodwill.

Unlike many of the places we have lived, while in the Charlotte area, we made it a point to get out and explore the Carolinas --- from the piedmont to the coast. From Ashville to Raleigh and from Hilton Head to Myrtle Beach, we thoroughly enjoyed the sightseeing, golf, local cuisine, conversation and the precious time we spent together. Our decision to respond to the circumstance which surfaced as a result of a shorter stay in Ohio than we expected, not only added to our confidence of being able to earn a living outside of corporate America but also contributed significantly to the overall richness in our life.

Because we were aware of who we were at this time as a couple and what was important to us, we mustered the courage to shape an outcome which had dimensions of richness far beyond just replacing an income source.

CHAPTER NINETEEN

JOINING THE BETTERLIVING™ FAMILY

MODAL EXPLORATION

Discovery

The spring of 2004 was a time of personal reflection and professional frustration for both of us. Earl, as the CEO of Maryland-based MedContrax, had completed the unrewarding chore of leading the company into a strategic alignment with an industry rival. The asset merger was necessitated by MedContrax's inability to close a second round of venture capital funding following the September 11, 2001 terrorist attack.

Cobb's home at Harroway at the Lakes in 2004.

He had returned back to our home in Charlotte, NC later that year. He was currently working as an executive consultant for a Charlotte-based management consulting firm as well as working as an adjunct professor of management at DeVry University's Keller Graduate School of Management.

We had sold our General Nutrition Center (GNC) franchise in the fall of 2003. Due to a sublease issue with the franchisor, we agreed to a legal settlement which allowed us to sell the franchise back to GNC at a premium. However, the primary disappointment of the entire GNC experience was our relationship as a franchisee with the GNC corporate office. The company had recently been purchased by a new ownership group. The ownership change seemed to also bring a change of management philosophy. GNC corporate managers appeared to no longer be as supportive of their 2000 franchise locations as they were of their 2000 corporate owned stores. From competing pricing to conflicting information regarding product shelf life, the list of issues [being experienced by many GNC franchise owner/operators] grew to the point where we realized that maintaining the relationship with GNC as a franchisee was not in our best interest.

During this time, I was doing freelance work as a part of our CobbCare Consulting business. We had sold the lake house a year earlier and had purchased another wonderful home in the Lake Norman area not far from the old Sterling Point location. The new house was in a development known as Harroway at the Lakes. With over 3,000 sq. ft. of living space, we each had home offices on the second floor and managed to coexist peacefully as we logged long workdays.

Even though we were busy and financially stable, we both felt that we were not fully utilizing our talents and still had an "itch" to be CEOs of our own company.

Following a visit to North Carolina by our daughter, Brandi, and her first child early in 2004, we began to more seriously discuss why we felt the need to get involved in another business start-up at this time. Initially, we admitted to ourselves that our situation had the makings of a true *conundrum*. But, after several weeks of back-and-forth dialogue, we began to analyze the situation more thoroughly. We wanted to finally get our minds around what was driving us to desire another entrepreneurial episode in our life.

For me, I concluded that through the CobbCare GNC experience, I had demonstrated that I had what it takes to generate and execute a marketing plan and drive the operations of a business to consistent profitability. But, more importantly, through the experience, I found that growing a small business which completely embodied my own values and personality was much more satisfying than many of the multi-million dollar deals I was involved in during my investment banking days.

Earl mostly talked about how immensely he enjoyed his leadership position with MedContrax and was intrigued by the contrast it provided as compared to his extensive experience in leading major businesses within Fortune 500 companies. We had just celebrated his 50th birthday --- a celebration which included a James Bond themed party I hosted at our home and attended by over fifty friends, family members and well-wishers --- and was becoming more and more anxious about the window of time available to him to build upon his venture experience.

It seemed that both of us, particularly after Brandi's visit, were beginning to feel more strongly about addressing our need to take another *shot* at establishing a family enterprise. It was our long time goal to eventually establish a viable business which would be available for our daughter and grandchildren to leverage as they carved out the next generation of livelihoods for themselves and their families.

As a consequence of this situational analysis, we surprisingly found that multiple events in our lives over the past several years [most resulting in positive outcomes] had generated an undeniable circumstance which had surfaced at this time in our life.

Our Circumstance: Although we find ourselves busy and financially stable, we are still driven to respond to an intense desire to get involved in another business start-up. Our desire seems to encompass a combination of being at a stage in life where we are not fully utilizing our extensive business development experience and an acute sensation almost certainly caused by having been bitten again by the "entrepreneurial bug". Since we are both around 50 years old, we would probably also be deciding whether or not we would ever again get involved in a significant new business startup.

Our Opportunity: If we decide to get involved in another business startup at this time, we could set the company's growth on a trajectory such that we could target retirement and getting young family members involved in the business within the next ten years. The idea of establishing an enterprise which would be available for our daughter, grandchildren, nieces and nephews to leverage in support of their livelihoods has been a long time goal. With the financial resources, good health and burning desire currently available to invest in the right business --- now might be our *best shot* at succeeding and reaching this goal.

Deliberation

Prior to selecting the appropriate response to our circumstance, we must first determine how we would select and assess a business which would generate significant annual revenue and have the potential to appreciate in value in the long term. Because of the magnitude of the financial investment that would be required, we felt that we should spend the time upfront to clearly understand the most critical aspects of such a business venture. After considerable deliberation, we concluded that the following three areas encompassed those aspects:

- We should outline the attributes of the type of business which would best provide us with what we would enjoy doing on a daily basis, the level of challenge we required and a means of achieving our longer term expectations.

Earl and I both agreed that our next business enterprise must have three key attributes.

The first was that the business must have the potential to generate three to five million dollars of annual revenue. This level of sales revenue was important. Within this range we could expect to net a five figure income and still have assets to invest in and grow the business. Most likely this would rule out a typical consulting type start-up which would be limited to the number of hours we could work. It would probably require that we either deliver a large volume of low-to-moderate priced products/services on an annual basis or ship a smaller number of higher priced items.

Secondly, the business must complement our combination of skills and interests. I would be most interested in a business which required a lot of customer touch and provided products and/or services which could, to some degree, be customized to meet the customer's individual needs. I also would enjoy a good marketing and creative advertising challenge. I knew that Earl, with his technical and operations management background, would be most interested in developing product and/or service delivery strategies, designing operational processes and working directly with the customers to ensure their total satisfaction.

Thirdly, the business must be one in which the operating model requires it to build and retain a significant amount of equity or value over time. Having spent a number of years operating smaller businesses to this point, we both realized that the facts are such that you live off the cash flow and you retire by selling the business or leveraging the retained equity.

- We should develop a "short list" of potential business categories that possessed such attributes. Then, conduct an assessment of each to determine the best candidate at this time.

Prior to this point, we had owned and operated two rather significant-sized small businesses in the Charlotte, NC area. In addition to a General Nutrition Center franchise which provided a well-defined operating format, we had also launched a business that we actually designed and built from "scratch" named Transit Express. Transit Express was a next-day and regional package delivery business that we opened in the spring of 2000 during the peak of the dot-com era. The sales were driven by major contracts with companies like Federal Express, Sears and Owens-Corning. Transit Express had a customer base of over 100 daily-use business customers across Mecklenburg County. After the business grew into an enterprise which included four company-owned 24/7 vans, a number of rental trucks, twelve employees and a warehouse, we sold the entire unit, as is, to a regional cargo logistics company based on an offer we could not refuse.

Therefore, along with the larger business units we had managed while in corporate America, we also had hands-on experience with smaller businesses with varying operating formats. Based on these experiences, we had a fairly good idea of the type of business that would meet our requirements for this new venture. So, we spent several weeks developing a list of potential business opportunities. Our research included working with business brokers, perusing the Wall Street Journal and other leading ad spots and surfing numerous websites. Generating the initial list was not much of a problem. However, getting this list down to what could be called a "short list" was the real challenge. We were leaning more toward businesses with a proven operating format, quality products/services and an excellent reputation based on customer referrals. We did not want another enterprise that we had to start from scratch. We had carved our list down to three real possibilities, but needed to make a final decision fairly quickly.

We finally decided, based on a trip to Souderton, Pennsylvania, that the best candidate possessing all of the attributes we had established and was within our "investment reach" was a Betterliving™ Patio and Sunrooms dealership being offered by a fifty year old company named Craft-Bilt Manufacturing.

Craft-Bilt was the leading sunroom manufacturer in the United States. The company also was the country's fastest growing manufacturer of awnings, canopies and solar shades. Other Craft-Bilt products included screen rooms, patio covers and fully engineered building panels. We were being offered a dealership which would cover 19 counties in the piedmont of North and South Carolina. Craft-Bilt's business model for their Betterliving™ dealerships was based on building high-quality, custom designed products at reasonable prices. Their sales and advertising strategy was fueled by targeted television infomercials. The Betterliving™ dealer sales, marketing and production training appeared to be among the best in the industry. Even though the strength of the patio and sunroom product was "construction", the heart of the business was marketing and sales. The average room sale could range from $15,000 to $40,000 and most customers brought their own financing via cash or home equity.

Thus, a Betterliving™ Patio and Sunrooms dealership appeared to meet all of the business attributes we required --- A marketing and sales driven, high quality, high ticket, low volume, skills-based, customer-oriented business with a protected territory large enough to build significant enterprise equity over time.

- We should develop a business plan which is realistic and capable of being executed within the investment and time limits we would establish.

This is where I turned to Earl and said "go for it". Earl had developed such a knack for thinking through and "operationalizing" business plans. When we first moved to the Charlotte, NC area he assisted me with the GNC franchise business plan. Of course, it was his plan that was the impetus behind Transit Express. He had also developed plans for several local groups in the region, ranging from aspiring entrepreneurs to seasoned business veterans.

Earl worked with Craft-Bilt Manufacturing's Director of Business Development to validate many of the assumptions surrounding every aspect of the business. Craft-Bilt provided typical cost-to-price ratios as well as the demographics around the customer base and average room sales. Since Earl would be the one to manage the operations/production end of the business, he spent a lot of time thinking through the cost of hiring and training a quality room construction staff. The plan would be to initially ramp up slowly. However, the plan must ensure that quality construction techniques and customer schedules were consistently maintained. Since I would be responsible for sales and marketing, I provided the required staffing plans and cost estimates in these areas.

After we reviewed the final version of the document and walked through several "what if" scenarios, we both felt that we had developed a realistic plan. *We still had to convince ourselves that a Charlotte-based business could be executed as planned and whether or not we could reach and surpass "breakeven" with the level of investment we would be willing to put into the endeavor.*

The two main questions that were still keeping us up at night were: Will a sufficient number of suitable in the Piedmont region of the Carolinas support a sunroom addition and would the television advertising dollars in the business plan be sufficient to attract the number of leads we would need to build and maintain a sustainable volume of orders?

Selection

Following another visit to the Craft-Bilt Manufacturing facility in Pennsylvania and some very candid and open conversations with the company's President, we had to make a decision. Not just on Craft-Bilt, but whether or not we really wanted to respond to the circumstance we were facing by engaging in another business startup at this time. After taking a few days away from it all and enjoying a weekend in Myrtle Beach, we decided to give another business start-up a *shot*.

The selection was really based on a number of reasons. We were convinced that the Betterliving™ dealership was an excellent match for us at this stage of our life. We would bring a tremendous amount of business experience and passion to a business based on a model that was working for scores of other dealers across the United States. The relationship we were developing with Craft-Bilt the

Earl and Charlotte in a Conference photo with other Owners of Betterliving™ Patio and Sunroom Dealerships in 2005.

company and Craft-Bilt the *people* felt comfortable. However, deciding to *join the Betterliving™ family* really came down to us both feeling that now was the time to take a *shot* at succeeding and reaching a long time goal. We optimistically named this new business venture *Project Better-Future*.

Engagement

The spring of 2004 was spent negotiating the terms of the Betterliving™ dealership agreement with Craft-Bilt and finalizing our business plan. We began to execute our plan within weeks after executing the agreement. In August 2005, we held the grand opening of *Betterliving™ Patio and Sunrooms of Central Carolinas*. I concentrated on adapting the standard administrative, marketing and sales processes to our dealership. Earl focused most of his attention on hiring a skilled construction team, attending the required installation training and obtaining the vehicles & equipment we would need to launch operations.

The months leading up to the dealership opening were full of long days. It was during this period that we also unearthed the first of several significant surprises.

What follows is an outline of the most significant milestones, activities and decisions associated with *Project Better-Future*.

- Fortunately, at the time we signed our dealership agreement with Craft-Bilt there was not a dealership fee. However, we were responsible for all expenses associated with establishing the enterprise in the Carolinas. To finance the dealership, we estimated that we would need to invest around $100,000 to cover the initial cost of facilities, vehicles, tools, equipment, insurance, training and staffing. Beyond the initial investment, we were prepared to inject up to another $150,000 to support other capital requirements and to assist with cash flow during the ramp-up phase of the business.

- By opening the dealership in August, we accepted the risk of not having a longer summer sales period to aid in building a backlog of orders. Summer was the most active sales period for dealerships in the North and East. However, we felt that in the South the fall and even the early winter weather was still fairly pleasant. Thus, the constraints on outside construction were not as severe as in other parts of the country.

- Prior to the August 2005 grand opening, we completed a long list of milestones. To this day, we are not sure how we successfully accomplished so many critical and somewhat challenging activities in this timeframe. Among them were:

    o We worked with a local bank and credit union to establish the banking and line of credit relationships we would need to support the business operations.

    o We worked with an insurance broker to purchase the compulsory levels of hazard and workers compensation insurance. We also worked with a health insurance company and purchased an affordable policy to cover all full time employees.

    o We worked with the City of Charlotte and Mecklenburg County to secure the licenses and bonds required to operate a construction business in the region.

    o With the assistance of Earl's brother Andrew, a retired HR executive, we developed and published a complete set of Human Resources, Employee Conduct and Company Benefits manuals.

    o We advertised in the local paper and hired our first two skilled carpenters, one experienced sales person and an office manager/administrative assistant.

    o We worked with a commercial real estate broker to identify a facility to launch our initial operations. The Craft-Bilt facility recommendations included a 1,000 to

2,000 sq. ft. showroom to display some completed products as well as a warehouse ranging from 4,000 to 5,000 sq. ft. to maintain vehicles and sunroom construction materials.

- We started a 12-week course to prepare both us to take the North and South Carolina Contractors Examination to become licensed contractors in the two states.

- We purchased a new sub-compact car for sales calls and two new Ford F-250 trucks. We equipped the trucks with ladder racks, tools boxes and the required aluminum brake. Earl purchased all of the construction tools and warehouse fixtures required to safely install the custom built sunrooms.

- Earl and the carpenters attended a two week training course at the Craft-Bilt facility in Pennsylvania to become certified in designing and building both the standard and vinyl version of the rooms. To Earl's surprise, he was selected as top in his class based on written exams and actual construction demonstrations that were a part of the intense training. All of the Betterliving™ patio and sunrooms were constructed on-site. They were engineered structures consisting of cut-to-order extruded aluminum along with custom glass, doors and window components.

- Both Earl and I attended the week long sales class at the Craft-Bilt facility along with our new sales person. A significant part of successfully installing a Betterliving™ sunroom was ensuring that the room design met both the homeowner's expectations as well as the engineered room installation specifications. In other words, all room designs were not suited for all home layouts. There was also the need for exact measurements and other design features such as building code requirements for all existing or new decks and concrete slab foundations. The sales person's product knowledge and installation measurement skills were all critical to these aspects of the room sales and design process.

- The most challenging and what turned out to be the most revealing set of activities were associated with the selection of an adequate facility from which to initially launch the Betterliving™ Patio and Sunrooms of Central Carolinas enterprise. As mentioned above, Craft-Bilt management had specific recommendations for its Betterliving™ dealerships. We spent several days touring prospective locations and facilities with the Craft-Bilt President prior to the August 2005 grand opening. Earl spent a week traveling to existing Betterliving™ Patio and Sunrooms locations in the mid-west. The most recent Betterliving™ dealer expansions had occurred in the Milwaukee and Chicago areas. He toured the facilities and discussed start-up strategy with the other Betterliving™ dealers.

- You might not call it a *sixth-sense* but neither Earl nor I felt comfortable with this aspect of the start-up. We both were very concerned about entering into a four or five year commercial lease for 5,000 to 6,000 sq. ft. of office, showroom and warehouse space. We felt that we needed a better sense of how the Betterliving™ business model would work in the Carolinas market prior to making that level of financial commitment. To this point, Craft-Bilt had only provided us general information regarding the Charlotte area market for sunroom additions and infomercial sales techniques.

- However, as luck or fate would have it, during our new hire interview process, we learned that our new sales person and one of our installers had actually worked for a Betterliving™ dealer who had operated in the Charlotte area. It appeared that the dealership had closed only a few years prior. This was news to us. During numerous meeting and discussions with Craft-Bilt, we were not provided any meaningful information regarding a prior dealer in the territory.

- Then, we experienced another revealing episode while touring potential facilities with the Craft-Bilt President prior to making a decision. The real estate broker was showing us a building located in a business park in North Charlotte. After getting a description of the type of business we would be operating, the broker indicated he wanted to show us another building. He rushed us over to another location in the same office park. He excitedly showed us a space which had an office area, a showroom and a 5,000 sq. ft. warehouse area. The building had not been leased since the previous tenant vacated the property. The broker recalled that the previous tenant stored extruded aluminum beams in the warehouse area. Earl and I looked at each other and then at the Craft-Bilt President.

- Following the tour and while enjoying some Carolina pulled-pork for lunch, Craft-Bilt confirmed that the building we had just seen was the location of the prior Betterliving™ dealer. The previous dealer was also based in the Charlotte area and had the same territory we had just agreed to service with Betterliving™ products. This discovery was quite revealing.

Certainly, we would now request all of the historical performance data available regarding the previous dealership and factor this insight into our business plan and overall operations strategy. But, learning of the prior dealer and this location in this manner moved us to a cautious and more observant state-of-mind regarding all aspects of *Project Better-Future*. We were sure that it was a location that the Craft-Bilt President and business development director had visited a number of times in the past, yet they failed to mention it to us in previous discussions.

Betterliving Patio & Sunrooms of the Central Carolinas location in 2005.

- In August 2005, we proudly opened the Betterliving™ Patio and Sunrooms of Central Carolinas located at 714 Montana Avenue. The 2,000 sq. ft. building was located in a small office park. We were able to lease this corner unit from a neighbor who was also a prior landlord. The building was located just off of I-85 and Beatties Ford Road in Charlotte, NC. It had easy access to both I-85 and to I-77. It was large enough to contain a nice office area and a small warehouse. The warehouse was organized such that we could maintain, at the minimum, sufficient material to support up to five room orders. Surprisingly, we could also store the company trucks in the warehouse at night.

Betterliving™ Patio and Sunrooms of Central Carolinas' first sunroom project.

- Between August and November 2005 we successfully sold and built new patio and sunrooms. The first room we completed was actually in the state of Virginia. We agreed to sub-build the room with the Betterliving™ dealer in the area to give our new carpenter/installers some early experience with the more complicated gable designed rooms. Our construction sites ranged from locations in older and more established Charlotte neighborhoods to new outlying sub-divisions. We built rooms to the north in the Raleigh, NC area and down toward the coast in the prestigious Pinehurst area.

Charlotte displaying new products.

- As we moved into the winter, business began to slow down. We expected the winter months to be slower and had budgeted to retain all of our employees. However, we did not expect the level of increase in the cost of advertising. We also were surprised by the changes that had occurred in the local telemarketing environment.

- The majority of the sales leads in this type of business format were generated from calls received from potential customers immediately after viewing our infomercials. The cost of these types of television broadcasts vary from city to city and are based on broadcast times. In the metropolitan Charlotte market, the cost per minute had increased significantly over the past decade.

- The number of leads received per broadcast could be historically tied to the number of customer home visits [where 95% of room sales are made and orders taken] and the number of rooms sold. This is why we had always viewed this business as being more of a "numbers game" or a sales/marketing challenge versus a construction business.

- As we approached the spring of 2006, we were spending more and more of our budget to purchase infomercials and receiving fewer and fewer sales leads per broadcast. I recall going into the office on a Sunday morning after an $800 Saturday night infomercial broadcast and finding only two phone requests for more information. That equaled $400 per lead. Ouch.

- In addition to the increase in "cost per sales lead" we noticed an equally troublesome and unexpected telemarketing reality. With the advent of caller ID, a higher percentage of calls returned to the potential customers by our sales staff [to schedule customer home visits] were going unanswered. Typically, we would attempt to return a call responding to an inquiry as many as 10-15 times in an attempt to make contact. This follow-up activity, in itself, was becoming a more costly, but necessary, business function. We began discussions with Craft-Bilt in March 2006 regarding the need for assistance in deciphering the current Charlotte, NC sales and media market. To our dismay, we were not provided the type of support we were expecting. We had expected some fresh ideas such as hosting a local focus group to

Earl on the showroom floor.

gain a better understanding of the current market. We also thought that it would be appropriate to revise some of the infomercials in an attempt to attract a broader set of potential consumers.

- With Craft-Bilt continuing only to recommend that we "invest more money in the same infomercials" and the fact that new print advertising was not working, we found ourselves with another potential *conundrum*. Except at this point in time, we had a couple of hundred thousand reasons to solve this riddle. The inevitable outcome would not only impact our life, but also the lives of employees and customers with whom we had taken deposits for pending orders.

- After a difficult strategy meeting in mid-April 2006, Earl and I met with our staff and shared our plan. We would make a significant investment in both television and print advertising. We would also increase the sales support effort between April and June. If we were able to obtain the business results we needed, we would target the items that worked and lay out broader plans to achieve the remainder of the year's goals. If we did not see improvement in results, we would be forced to *pull the plug* on current business operations and make a decision regarding future business options.

Outcomes

Earl's niece, Glory and Sales Staff supporting a Home and Garden Show marketing exhibit.

As we approached mid-May, it was becoming more and more obvious that the Carolinas market was, again, not a good one for a Betterliving™ Patio and Sunrooms dealership. Even with a significant increase in both television and print advertising, we were not able to realize the increase in orders we needed to justify additional investment. Earl shared with me an old adage that his father had shared with him when he was a young boy --- *"When you find yourself in a hole that's getting deeper and deeper with no apparent way out, then stop digging"*

Thus, in May of 2006 we began to take the necessary and prudent actions to shut down the operations of Betterliving™ Patio and Sunrooms of Central Carolinas. We were committed to completing all of the sunroom installations we had in backlog. We made sure that all of our customers were satisfied with their purchases. We also provided all of our employees with a severance package. The package included all outstanding vacation pay, two-weeks of salary and a COBRA option to maintain their healthcare policy. We paid off or worked out agreements with all of our venders. Having selected a month-to-month facility lease, we were able to navigate a rather soft landing.

Without question, *Project Better-Future* turned out to be a project unfulfilled. However, it was not an experience without important lessons learned.

Even though our objective of establishing an enterprise which would be available for our family to leverage in support of their livelihoods had not been realized, the wherewithal, courage and passion required to take a *shot at a dream* was demonstrated.

During *Project Better-Future,* several family members were involved in the business operations. We also had the support and involvement of some dear friends. I am reminded of the words of an unknown author who pinned, *"Dreams are like stars, you may never touch them, but if you follow them they will lead you to your destiny."*

While Earl and I were wrapping up the closure of the patio and sunroom business and contemplating what might be next in our life, we were somewhat surprised when opportunities for both of us to return to Arizona surfaced. Returning to Arizona at that time would also put us in the position to get to know our young grandchildren. Our daughter had her hands full with a 5 year old and 10 month old. Within a matter of months, we found ourselves on another one of our life journeys as we returned to the Sonoran desert.

Thoughts Regarding Our Exploration

We had responded [and not simply reacted] to another major circumstance in our life. By implementing *Project Better-Future*, we had followed through on our objective to shape the best outcome to an undeniable circumstance. On one hand, we experienced a negative --- we lost money. Yet, on the other hand by recognizing when to "cut our losses" we may have significantly minimized a broader negative impact.

Nevertheless, by knowing that life is a continuum and not a collection of random events, we were *not surprised* that the years we spent together subsequent to *Project Better-Future* were more loving and the relationships we developed with our grandsons turned out to be *priceless*.

Maybe without our knowledge, we were not just building sunrooms but also following the stars which would eventually lead to *our destiny*.

PART IV

NAVIGATING THE LIFE ENRICHMENT MODEL™

THE LIFE ENRICHMENT MODEL™

APPLICATION GUIDE

IMPORTANT: READ THIS BEFORE STARTING YOUR FIRST PROJECT

Use this Guide to apply the *Life Enrichment Model*™ to major events and the resulting circumstances that you may encounter in your life. Just follow the directions as set forth within each section. You should begin your project with Section 1.0, *The Framing Stage*.

You should not attempt to complete this project in one sitting. You should give yourself time to thoughtfully complete each section. It would be helpful to involve others, i.e. family members, friends, a professional coach or someone you trust, to be a part of what should be a confidential evaluation, analysis and course of action. Honest feedback from others can be extremely helpful in order to gain a more complete and healthier perspective of your circumstance. A complete or comprehensive view of all aspects of your situation is essential to confirming the facts surrounding the event.

You should give your project a name, i.e. *Project Make It Happen*. This will help to remind you that it also needs your attention as you go about other important daily tasks.

Your goal is to clearly and thoroughly understand your situation, your options and the potential consequences of your action or inaction. You should think through all the circumstances and potential opportunities that may be available to shape a more positive outcome.

Remember to consider all of your personal, professional and spiritual gifts as well as other resources that can be brought to bear to this situation. You should properly address all of the circumstances you are facing as a result of the event. Be mindful of what it will take to seize the potential opportunities and whether or not you are up to the task at this time.

Be diligent about planning the tasks and activities required to generate the desired outcomes. You must follow through on what must be done. Give this project the focus and priority it deserves. By starting and completing this project, we are sure you will make better decisions, feel better about the outcomes and experience the addition of richness in your life.

If we can be of any assistance with personal one-on-one coaching [via email, teleconference or in person], do not hesitate to contact us. There may also be opportunities for you to attend a local presentation or a group workshop in your area. You can find information on RICHER LIFE presentations and workshops at www.richerlifeassociates.com.

We wish you the best as you strive to get the most out of your gifts and circumstances. By doing so, you are on your way to living a richer life.

Application Guide

Project Name_____   Date Started_____

1.0 The Framing Stage

Goal:	To extract a view or *frame* of your mind-set in order to reveal how you can place yourself in the best position to identify and examine opportunities embedded within a circumstance.
Input:	Review of the five stages of the Life Enrichment Model™ and detail descriptions of each model component to become familiar with their role in the modeling process.
Output:	An approximation of your current *perspective*. It is believed that this *approximation* is consistent with the "probable mind-set" you will take into your evaluation of the event and circumstance at hand.
Model Components:	*Framing Process, Framing Elements* and the "*Framing Query*".

Application Steps:

1. Summarize your thoughts regarding your current view or perspective of the situation at hand.
2. Complete Framing Query (See "Framing Query" Reference Sheet).
3. Grade your Framing Query results to determine Enrichment Platform (See "Grading the Framing Query" Reference Sheet).
4. Examine the Archetypes associated with the Enrichment Platform as determined by the Framing Query results (See "Platform Archetypes" Reference Sheet.)
5. Evaluate the thoughts you recorded in step 1 now that you have reviewed the Platform Archetype and note how your perspective of the situation may have changed at this point.
6. Move to the next stage, Opportunity Identification.

Summary of my view and perspective of the situation at hand.

Changes in my perspective regarding the situation after the Framing Archetype review.

Application Guide

2.0 The Opportunity Identification Stage

Goal:	Evaluate each circumstance to identify embedded potential opportunities. Then analyze each potential opportunity to detail and document the desired outcomes.
Input:	A sufficient exposure to the characterizations and insights embodied within the *Platform Archetype* suggested by the Framing Query results. This will aid in ensuring that all characterizations represented by the Framing Elements all have a "top-of-mind" position.
Output:	A list of circumstances, embedded opportunities and desired outcomes associated with the situation you are facing along with the insight and awareness gained through the evaluation and analysis process.
Model Components:	Step-One of the TWO-STEP Opportunity Identification Methodology.

Application Steps:

1. Develop a list of circumstances, embedded opportunities and desired outcomes.
2. List ALL circumstances you perceive as apparent. Be specific and detail each opportunity and each desired outcome. Each circumstance should be unique but may be related to other circumstances.
3. Move to the next stage, Examination and Prioritization.

List of Circumstances	Potential Opportunities	Desired Outcomes
1.	1. 2 3.	1. 2 3.
2.	1. 2 3.	1. 2. 3.
4.	1. 2 3.	1. 2 3.
5.	1. 2 3.	1. 2 3.
6.	1. 2 3.	1. 2 3.

Application Guide

3.0 The Examination and Prioritization Stage

Goal:	To take the list of circumstances surrounding the situation at hand and decide which opportunities have the highest probability to enrich your life and are consistent with your capability to realize them at this time.
Input:	The list of "potential opportunities" developed during the Opportunity Identification Stage.
Output:	A list of the most actionable opportunities.
Model Components:	TWO-STEP Opportunity Identification Methodology and *Opportunity Priority Query*.

Application Steps:

1. *For each opportunity on your list, respond to each question of the Opportunity Priority Query. (See "Opportunity Priority Query" Reference Sheet)*
2. *Based on your response, select the most actionable opportunities which may shape a more positive outcome to the situation at hand.*
3. *Move to the next stage, Modal Exploration.*

Opportunity	Opportunity Priority Query Question #1		Opportunity Priority Query Question #2		Opportunity Priority Query Question #3		Actionable Opportunity?
1.	YES	NO	YES	NO	YES	NO	YES ☐ NO ☐
2.	YES	NO	YES	NO	YES	NO	YES ☐ NO ☐
3.	YES	NO	YES	NO	YES	NO	YES ☐ NO ☐
4.	YES	NO	YES	NO	YES	NO	YES ☐ NO ☐
5.	YES	NO	YES	NO	YES	NO	YES ☐ NO ☐
6.	YES	NO	YES	NO	YES	NO	YES ☐ NO ☐
7.	YES	NO	YES	NO	YES	NO	YES ☐ NO ☐
8.	YES	NO	YES	NO	YES	NO	YES ☐ NO ☐

Application Guide

4.0 The Modal Exploration Stage

Goal:	Examine the list of most "actionable opportunities" to decide to either respond to the circumstance by pursuing the opportunity or to respond to the circumstance with another approach.
Input:	List of actionable opportunities from the Examination and Prioritization Stage.
Output:	An action plan for seizing each opportunity to be pursued. NOTE: A decision not to pursue the opportunity concludes the exploration process.
Model Components:	Modal Exploration process.

Application Steps:

1. *Examine the list of actionable opportunities using the Modal Exploration Process (See "Modal Exploration Process" Reference Sheet)*
2. *During the "Selection" mode of the process decide to either pursue the opportunity or not.*
3. *In the "Engagement" mode develop an action plan which will generate the desired outcomes.*
4. *Move to the next stage, Action Execution.*

Actionable Opportunity	Exploration Mode	Objectives and Outcomes
1.	Discovery	
	Deliberation	
	Selection	
	Engagement	
2.	Discovery	
	Deliberation	
	Selection	
	Engagement	
3.	Discovery	
	Deliberation	
	Selection	
	Engagement	
4.	Discovery	
	Deliberation	
	Selection	
	Engagement	

Application Guide

5.0 The Action Execution Stage

Goal:	The Action Execution Stage tracks the execution of the actions developed and planned as a part of the Engagement Mode within the Modal Exploration Process.
Input:	Action Plan from Engagement Mode within the Modal Exploration Process.
Output:	Successful execution of actions required to address each circumstance and obtain the desired outcomes.
Model Components:	Engagement Mode within the Modal Exploration Process.

Application Steps

1. *Closely track the execution of all actions.*
2. *Note any follow-up actions that may be required.*

Action Item	Action Plan	Date Action Complete	Follow-up Actions
1.	• What • Who • Where • When • Desired result • Actual result		
2.	• What • Who • Where • When • Desired result • Actual result		
3.	• What • Who • Where • When • Desired result • Actual result		
4.	• What • Who • Where • When • Desired result • Actual result		

THE LIFE ENRICHMENT MODEL™

REFERENCE SHEETS

THE LIFE ENRICHMENT CONTINUUM™

The *Life Enrichment Continuum*™ is a paradigm that provides a systematic approach to characterizing [in a practical manner] the various environmental and human behavioral factors that come into play when any of us encounter circumstances in life.

The *Life Enrichment Continuum*™ is summarized in terms of its four basic *Enrichment Principles* and corresponding *Enrichment Challenges*.

Each Enrichment Principle sets forth a thought provoking observation regarding the environment and the forces at play when you find yourself in the position in life where you must encounter a potentially life altering circumstance. Integrating the Enrichment Principles into your *theater of thought* during these times will assist in establishing the *state of mind* optimum to properly identifying embedded enrichment opportunities.

The corresponding Enrichment Challenges constitute the knowledge-based objective or target you should attempt to achieve as you shape your responses to the circumstances which surround each event. Collectively, the Principles and Challenges establish the framework required to move you into position to get the most out of life's gifts and circumstances.

PRINCIPLES and CHALLENGES

ENRICHMENT PRINCIPLE No. 1 - As we travel along the *Continuum of Life*, from one stage to the next, we accumulate insights and experiences which alter how we perceive ourselves, how we perceive others and how we respond to opportunities for life enrichment.

> **Enrichment Challenge** - *To recognize life enrichment opportunities presented to us as we travel along the Continuum of Life and to leverage the experience, maturity and wisdom we have accumulated by shaping our behaviors, perceptions and responses in order to take advantage of these opportunities.*

ENRICHMENT PRINCIPLE No. 2 - Negative outcomes as a result of encountering a circumstance, at any time along the *Continuum of Life*, can and most often impede life enrichment. Positive outcomes have both near and long term impacts and, in most cases, significantly enhance the richness [quality, fullness and abundance] in our lives.

> **Enrichment Challenge** - *To leverage the refinement and growth of our humanistic gifts (qualities) as we travel along the Continuum of Life in order to facilitate as many positive outcomes and eliminate as many negative outcomes as possible.*

ENRICHMENT PRINCIPLE No. 3 – The measure of richness in our life is based on the societal norms of the day and is an omnipresent perception which significantly influences our behaviors and responses to life's challenges and circumstances.

> **Enrichment Challenge** - *To maintain an awareness and perspective of the norms that are in vogue within society and to establish our own individual measure and perception of richness in our life as we respond to life's challenges and circumstances.*

ENRICHMENT PRINCIPLE No. 4 – Positive outcomes which result from taking advantage of enrichment opportunities later in life may have the potential of significantly offsetting the impact of negative outcomes at earlier stages in our life.

> **Enrichment Challenge** - *To enrich our lives to the fullest, we must not only recognize enrichment opportunities embedded within life altering circumstances but we must also take the actions necessary to ensure that we fully realize [gain the full impact of] as many positive outcomes as possible.*

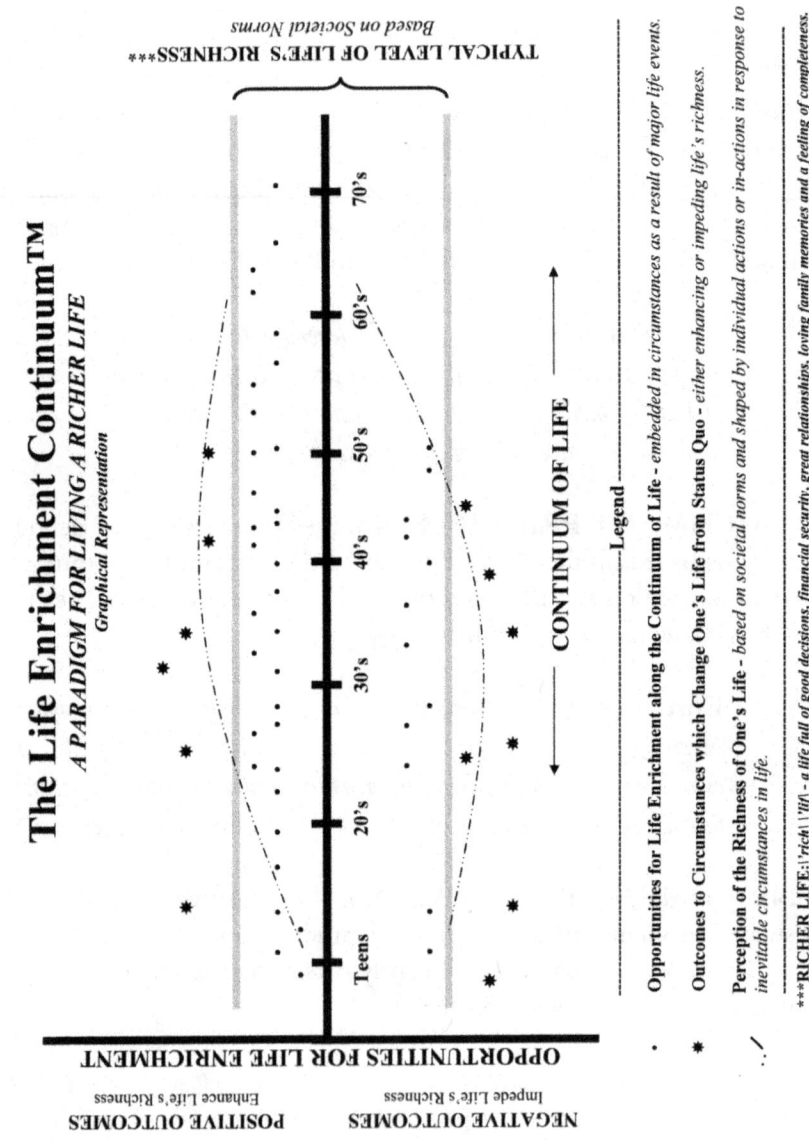

Life Enrichment Model™

When properly applied, the *Life Enrichment Model*™ can become an exceptional tool to aid in identifying unforeseen opportunities and determining the paths available to you as you encounter potentially life changing circumstances. The results of the model's queries can help you get into *the position* [both mentally and practically] to make better decisions, take appropriate actions and to more consciously make the adjustments required to formulate your responses to shape more positive outcomes.

The model's construct utilizes figurative depictions and characterizations to provide valuable insights into the intangibles in your life at the time you encounter a major circumstance. The depictions and characterizations are generalizations and should be used *as a guide* to steer you in a most probable direction. However, when you merge these *generalities* with your own timely [internal and external] observations and sound reasoning, this combination gives you a significant advantage as compared to simple *reacting* and *going it alone*.

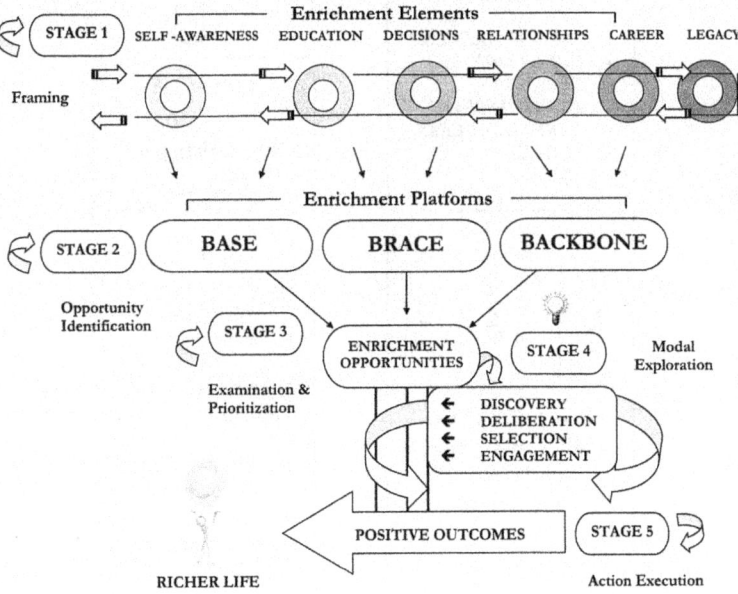

The Framing Process

The Framing Process systematically approximates your *mind-set* at the time you face major circumstances. The school of thought and general thesis of the *Framing* methodology is as follows:

"Your state of mind and perspective can be generally characterized by capturing an *inventory of your thoughts* surrounding six structural components, referred to as *Elements*. These *Elements* are believed to comprise an underlying system or structure that gives shape, strengthens and frames *who you are* and *what you are thinking* at the time you initially encounter a major circumstance in your life."

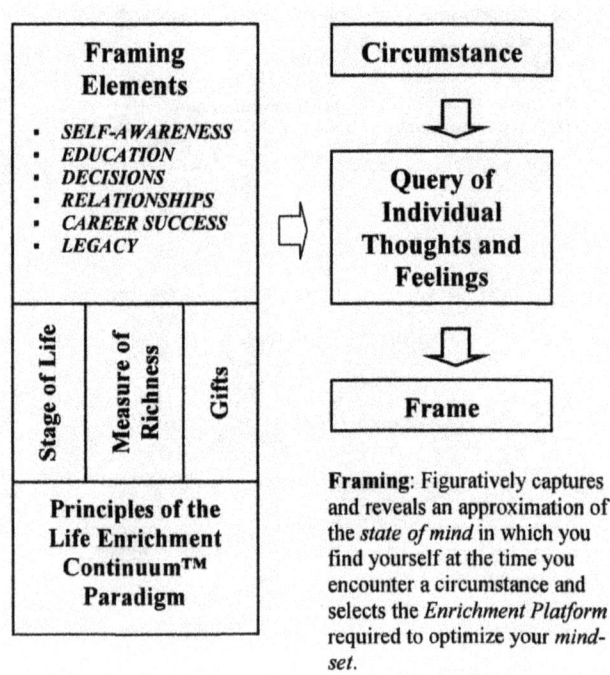

Framing: Figuratively captures and reveals an approximation of the *state of mind* in which you find yourself at the time you encounter a circumstance and selects the *Enrichment Platform* required to optimize your *mind-set*.

The Framing Query

Provide "Best Answer" to each question below by responding with either True(T) or False(F)

Questions	Response (Circle one)	
1. Being self-aware allows me to recognize my emotions and their effects on my life.	True	False
2. Self-awareness limits my ability to accept candid feedback.	True	False
3. Even with a high level of self-awareness it is difficult to be confident about a situation when there are uncertainties and pressures involved.	True	False
4. Being self-aware means knowing more about others and how they view me.	True	False
5. A lower level of self-awareness makes it easier for others to understand me.	True	False
6. Having an accurate sense of who I am helps me decide what areas in my life I should improve.	True	False
7. Self-awareness helps to know my strengths but not cope with my weaknesses.	True	False
8. My emotional self-awareness makes me a more effective and intuitive decision maker.	True	False
9. Education is the knowledge of putting our potentials to maximum use.	True	False
10. It is not possible to be a life-long learner as you get older.	True	False
11. Learning is best done in the classroom.	True	False
12. There is more to good education than just demonstrating reading, writing, listening and speaking skills.	True	False
13. Even with an education, it still may not be possible to understand and remember new information.	True	False
14. I find it easy to adapt new methods to move forward.	True	False
15. I have obtained all of the education I need to be successful in life.	True	False
16. Life long learners are generally college educators with multiple degrees.	True	False
17. Generally, options are limited in most circumstances.	True	False
18. When options are limited I make decisions quickly since things most likely will not change.	True	False
19. I should always make a list of every possible outcome to all major circumstances I encounter.	True	False
20. I should never trust my intuition when making a difficult decision.	True	False
21. If I am not gifted in an area of competence that will help me make a better decision, I will make a good guess instead of bothering someone that I trust.	True	False
22. When it is difficult to choose between two options, I most often choose the one that is supported by both logic and intuition.	True	False
23. I should not focus on drawing insight and wisdom from every decision I make.	True	False
24. I do not have to feel comfortable with a decision if it is the correct one.	True	False
25. There are many qualities that make up positive and valuable relationships.	True	False

26.	Because most relationships are so complex, you have to accept what you get.	True	False
27.	I should always attempt to grow, leverage and maintain positive, valuable relationships.	True	False
28.	My interpersonal skills are important but not critical to a good relationship.	True	False
29.	I should concern myself with the impact of my decisions only if they involve family members and close friends.	True	False
30.	Knowing too much about others makes it difficult to grow a quality and positive relationship since there is little to learn and discover.	True	False
31.	A good relationship does not have any give-and-take when it comes to tackling challenging circumstances.	True	False
32.	I should take full responsibility for learning as much about the other person as possible.	True	False
33.	I am only partially responsible for my career because I will always need help from others.	True	False
34.	Having a successful career is not one of the most important factors in achieving my life goals.	True	False
35.	In order to keep my career on track, I must continuously update my skills and knowledge.	True	False
36.	Your current job or position is never the best place to start from when you are trying to move your career forward.	True	False
37.	If required, I have the power and determination to re-invent my career.	True	False
38.	A network of colleagues and acquaintances is good, but not a necessary part of managing my career and finding the best opportunities for advancement.	True	False
39.	You should always be prepared for the next opportunity.	True	False
40.	A successful career will be free of all negatives and disappointments.	True	False
41.	My overall success in life will define the future success of my legacy.	True	False
42.	There are only a few good reasons for valuing and leaving a legacy.	True	False
43.	Most people do not require some kind of assistance from others.	True	False
44.	To leave a legacy I simply need to give a gift to a charity.	True	False
45.	If I give to private foundations, I lose all personal control of who gets my help.	True	False
46.	Community foundations only accept large cash donations.	True	False
47.	A community foundation can pool funds and achieve economies of scale for investing, managing and granting philanthropic dollars.	True	False
48.	The act of giving itself reinforces who we are as human beings.	True	False

Grading the Framing Query and Selecting Archetypes

Step# [1] Place your responses in Column #2			Step# [2]	Step# [3]	Step# [4]	Step# [5]
Question #	Your Response (T or F)	Answer Key	Place a "X" next to the answers which match the Answer Key.	Total the number of "X's" for each of the three groups and place total in Box	Rank from 1 to 3 the "Totals" from Step #3 (With "1" being the highest total and "3" the lowest total).	Thoroughly review the Archetypes below associated with the LOWEST RANKED Group in Step # 4. This will optimize your *mind-set* prior to moving to the Opportunity Identification Stage.
1		T				
2		F				
3		F				
4		F			(If you have a "TIE ", review all Archetypes)	
5		F				
6		T				Platform: BASE
7		F				*Platform Archetypes*
8		T		☐	( )	**Awareness Anchor**
9		T				and
10		F				**Education Enthusiast**
11		F		TOTAL	Group A RANK	
12		T				
13		F				
14		T				
15		F				
16		F				
17		F				
18		F				
19		T				
20		F				
21		T				Platform: BRACE
22		T				*Platform Archetypes*
23		T				**Decisions Dynamo**
24		F		☐	( )	and
25		T				**Relationship Rancher**
26		F			Group B	
27		T		TOTAL	RANK	
28		F				
29		F				
30		F				
31		F				
32		T				
33		F				
34		F				
35		T				
36		F				
37		T				Platform: BASE
38		F				*Platform Archetypes*
39		T				**Career Carver**
40		F		☐	( )	and
41		T				**Legacy Leaver**
42		F			Group B	
43		F		TOTAL	RANK	
44		F				
45		F				
46		F				
47		T				
48		T				

Opportunity Priority Query

1. Do I have the physical, psychological & intellectual strength and stamina to take on what is required to move this situation, from where it is today, to where I envision it has to be, in order to obtain the value & richness I perceive it will add to my life, when fully realized?

	YES
	NO

If No: Why Not? What are your concerns?

2. Do I have or can I acquire the level of resources [financial, moral & spiritual] required to seize the opportunity?

	YES
	NO

If No: Why Not? What are your concerns?

3. If I decide to do nothing, am I ready to accept and live with the consequences that may arise as a result of this circumstance?

	YES
	NO

If No: Why Not? What are your concerns?

Two-Step Opportunity Identification Methodology

The TWO-STEP Opportunity Identification Methodology guides your thought process as you examine and prioritize opportunities and shape your responses to the circumstances. The methodology is designed to identify the most favorable starting point or optimal *platform* for entering into the opportunity examination process.

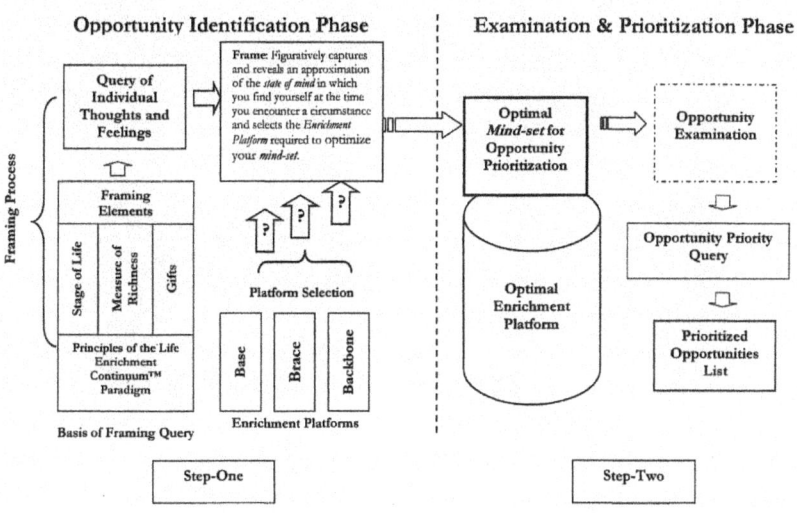

Modal Exploration

1.0 Discovery Mode

The circumstance(s) surrounding the event or situation are:

I can best describe the opportunity as follows:

2.0 Deliberation Mode

Summarize the tasks and activities that would be required to seize the opportunity and ensure the desired outcome.

I will need to do the following:

I need to get the following people involved for the reasons noted:

My concerns are as follows:

3.0 Selection Mode

Document the Pros and Cons associated with your ability to complete the tasks and activities required to seize the opportunity. After carefully weighing the Pros, Cons and your ability to execute what is required, then make a decision to either pursue the opportunity or to respond to the circumstance with another approach. A decision not to pursue the opportunity concludes the Modal Exploration process.

The Pros in this situation are as follows:

The Cons in this situation are as follows:

My Concerns with being able to do what is required to seize the opportunity are:

My Decision is:

Basis of my Decision is as follows:

4.0 Engagement and Action Execution Modes

Action	Responsibility	Date Started	Date Completed

Enrichment Platform: **BASE**
Enrichment Element: **SELF-AWARENESS**

ARCHETYPE
AWARENESS ANCHOR

I am the *Awareness Anchor*. I am emotionally aware. I clearly recognize my emotions and their effects. I know which emotions I feel and why. I recognize how my feelings affect my performance. I have a guiding awareness of my values and goals. I know my strengths and limits.

I am aware of my strengths and weaknesses. I am reflective. I learn from my experiences. I am open to candid feedback, new perspectives, continuous learning, and self-development. I am able to show a sense of humor and perspective about myself.

I am self-confident. I am sure about my self-worth and capabilities. I present myself with self-assurance. I have "presence". I can voice views that are unpopular and go out on a limb for what is right. I am decisive. I am able to make sound decisions despite uncertainties and pressures.

I know that an essential factor in maintaining genuine personal connections with others is through my self-awareness. Through my self-awareness I have the ability to perceive what is going on with me at all times. Since skill of understanding who we are is not taught in school, achieving my level of self-awareness is an extremely difficult assignment.

I became the Awareness Anchor and learned the skill of becoming self-aware through a high level of focus and observation. However, it was my strong desire to attract and cultivate authentic, meaningful and satisfying personal relationships in my life that sustained the effort required to truly know myself.

Over the years, I have learned that the more I understand myself, the easier it is for others to understand me. This has set the stage for more meaningful, rewarding relationships in my life.

Having an accurate sense of who I am helps me decide what areas of my life I can improve. I am able to produce high quality decisions by knowing my strengths and how to cope with my weaknesses. I am not hesitant to consult colleagues and subordinates that I trust to both gain a broader perspective and understand unique details.

My emotional self-awareness allows me to become a more effective and intuitive decision maker. I am able to read my "gut feelings" and use this to help guide timely decisions when facing difficult circumstances. I know who I am at this moment. I am the *Awareness Anchor*.

Enrichment Platform: **BASE**
Enrichment Element: **EDUCATION**

ARCHETYPE
EDUCATION ENTHUSIAST

I am the *Education Enthusiast*. I am aware of the demands of the global workplace. I know the needs of society are changing rapidly. I believe that education, being the knowledge of putting our potentials to maximum use, is key to a productive lifestyle in the 21st century.

I believe that education is more than collecting knowledge without understanding its value. I believe that the processing of knowledge fuels inspiration, visionary ambitions, creativity, motivation and my ability to bounce back from failure. I believe that we all gain true value of knowledge through life-long learning.

I am a life-long learner. I use my strong reading, writing, listening and speaking skills to achieve my life goals. I possess an awareness of what I need to learn and know. I leverage my education and desire to learn to succeed in life by managing day-to-day circumstances. I have worked hard to become interdependent and interpersonally competent. I believe in persistence and responsibility.

It is in my nature to be venturesome and creative. I set specific goals for myself. I understand the value of adopting powerful strategies for attaining my goals. I closely monitor my performance for signs of progress. I am sensitive to the need to sometime restructure my physical and social environment to make it compatible with my goals. I efficiently manage my time. I find it easy to adapt new methods to move forward and build valuable relationships.

I know that it is important to be skilled in identifying, retrieving, and organizing information. I am capable of understanding and remembering new information. I proactively demonstrate critical thinking skills and my ability to reflect on my own understanding. I am self-directed. I am self-regulated. I am self-motivated. I am reflective.

I understand the value associated with being curious and motivated. I recognize the significance of being methodical and disciplined. I realize the power of being logical and analytical. Yet, I know the importance of being self-aware and flexible. When I come face-to-face with difficult circumstances, I carefully assess the situation and ask --- What can I learn?

I am the *Education Enthusiast.*

Enrichment Platform: **BRACE**
Enrichment Element: **DECISIONS**

ARCHETYPE
DECISIONS DYNAMO

I am the Decisions Dynamo. On my way to making good decisions I always list my options. It may appear that there is only one course of action, but I know that this is usually not true. Even if my situation seems limited, I always manage to identify alternatives.

I always weigh the possible outcomes to every major circumstance in my life. For every possible course of action, I list all possible outcomes. I then label them as either having a positive or negative impact on the richness of my life. One method I use to track this analysis is to place a plus sign (+) next to each positive outcome and a minus sign (-) next to each negative outcome.

I always consult my gift of intuition. If I am not gifted in an area which would help make a better decision, I will always seek input from someone I trust.

I must feel comfortable with all of the decisions I make. I will always make a decision and choose the best option available. I remind myself that making a final decision is always a difficult task. Thus, I focus first on the decisions on my list that are supported by both logic and intuition. My final choice always has more plus signs than negative signs and is always confirmed by my intuition.

I always monitor and evaluate the results and outcomes of my decisions. However, if I do not evaluate my decisions afterward, I will not learn anything from the experience. I need to know whether the outcome was what I expected. I need to know whether or not I would respond to the circumstance in the same way in the future.

In addition, I need to understand what I learned from each encounter with each circumstance.

As the Decisions Dynamo, I consistently focus on drawing insight and wisdom from every decision I make. My goal is always to ensure that every choice has a positive outcome.

Through my self-awareness, I know that regardless of my efforts, I may experience negative outcomes. However, I strive to always be aware of *what happened along the way*.

I am the *Decisions Dynamo*.

Enrichment Platform: **BRACE**
Enrichment Element: **RELATIONSHIPS**

ARCHETYPE
RELATIONSHIP RANCHER

I am the *Relationship Rancher*. There are many qualities that make up positive and valuable relationships. Good support, compromise and honest communication are just a few of the qualities I desire in all of my relationships. I believe in creating value in my life and contributing value to others.

My definition of value in a relationship includes the ability to grow, leverage and mutually benefit from the association. It also includes a balance between the ups and downs while expecting significantly more positives than negatives. I have learned that in order to grow, leverage and maintain positive, valuable relationships, I must first focus on developing my own relationship skills.

Strong relationship skills allow me to manage and always be in control of what I bring and what I take away from all my relationships. Over time, I have learned that what works best for me are strong communications, interpersonal, decision making and learning skills.

To sharpen my communications skills I speak so that others can understand me. That way, they do not have to guess what's important in my life and what I expect from a particular relationship. I listen actively so that I am sure I understand what's being shared and what's being asked of me. I strive for continuous improvement of my interpersonal skills.

I understand that I must cooperate with others and treat them in the same manner that I wish to be treated. I have found that I must work harder on improving my interpersonal skills as I advance in age and wisdom. It does not always pay to be the smartest person in the room. I am careful as well as cautious when it comes to decision-making. I take the time to clearly understand how my decisions will impact others. I am well aware of the need to give in order to receive. I am also mindful of the fact that all relationships are not equal. Sometimes the giving is to support one relationship and the value is returned by means of a different relationship.

I take full responsibility for learning as much about the other person as possible. The more I know about what each of us bring into a relationship the better I will be able to manage and control the unforeseen. I was taught early in life to really know someone, *make sure you are around for all four seasons*. I am very selective as to how I define and what I expect from my broad range of relationships. Each of my relationships has its three P's ---Place, Purpose and Position --- in my life.

In any relationship, there is going to be give-and-take as situations and circumstances change. Thus, I make sure that all my relationships are quality relationships. I make sure that they all are properly aligned with the richness I desire in my life. I am the *Relationship Ranger*.

Enrichment Platform: **BACKBONE**
Enrichment Element: **CAREER SUCCESS**

ARCHETYPE
CAREER CARVER

I am *Career Carver*. I know that in America today, more than ever, I am responsible for building my career and guiding it to the level of success that complements the richness I desire in my life.

I am a life-long learner. I know that one of the major factors for career success is to never stop learning. I know that my world is constantly changing and that just as in life, career success depends on identifying new ways of doing things. I know that in order to keep my career on track, I must continuously update my skills and knowledge.

I am a good listener. Because I am a good listener, I can learn things quickly and avoid many of the schools of hard knocks. I learn from other's experiences.

I know that my current job or position is the best place to start and move my career in the trajectory that I desire. I know that often very little separates the most successful people from the average person. I know that nothing comes free. I know that the best way to advance my career is to do my current job well and fulfill current responsibilities.

I am constantly building and adding to my network of colleagues and acquaintances. I know that my next career step might arise from my contact network. I spend quality time building new contacts and relationships. I never forget to maintain the relationships I already have.

I know that the best way to obtain valuable information from my network is to provide others with the information they are seeking. I am always prepared for the next opportunity. I maintain a current resume and update it regularly. I know that the next step on my career ladder to success may surface tomorrow.

But above all, when I find myself in a position where I am stalled in my career and my success is in jeopardy, I know that I have the power and determination to re-invent myself. I never lose sight of the fact that as we travel along the continuum of life, we will experience both negatives and positives in all phases of our life, including career success.

It is with this understanding that I know that true success in life is to increase positive outcomes and minimize negative outcomes. I know that, at times, success equals maintaining par for the course. I am *Career Carver.*

Enrichment Platform: **BACKBONE**
Enrichment Element: **LEGACY**

ARCHETYPE
LEGACY LEAVER

I am *Legacy Leaver*. I know that the key to success is to always start everything you do with an end in mind. I realize that this simple bit of common sense could really be applied to all aspects of life, including career, family, personal relationships and professional goals.

I believe that to live a life of passion and significance requires making noteworthy strives and achievements. As a legacy leaver, I express my personal values by integrating my charitable, family and financial goals.

I know that my overall success in life will define my legacy. I know that there are many reasons for valuing and leaving a legacy. Each is as important as the next. I see legacy giving as a responsibility owed to my community.

I know that most people require some kind of assistance, whether it's physical, financial or spiritual. I am well aware of local church congregation or food banks supplying meals during a tough time. I have seen how a scholarship has made a dream of college possible.

I have witnessed loved ones and friends receive compassionate care in local hospitals during illness or injury. As I travel along the continuum of life, I am reminded that more must be done to continue positive, humane acts of kindness and to sustain programs for personal enrichment.

I take advantage of a number of ways to be philanthropic. I feel good about living my life well and leaving a legacy.

I give to charitable organizations. My gifts to established charities provide direct support to those organizations such as schools, hospitals, arts and cultural institutions, human service agencies and religious organizations. My gifts to these nonprofit organizations vary in size. I give to private foundations. Private foundations allow me to retain personal control and flexibility over giving programs. My gifts to community foundations can be of any size, from as little as a dollar to thousands -- or millions -- of dollars. By pooling funds, community foundations achieve economies of scale for investing, managing and granting philanthropic dollars.

I know that when I give freely and without any expectations of a return, the act of giving itself reinforces who I am as a human being. I know that what I give unconditionally *will come back to me ten-fold* and will enrich my life. I am *Legacy Leaver.*

GLOSSARY OF TERMS

BACKBONE

BACKBONE is the third of the three Enrichment Platforms. It is the most substantial and sturdiest component within the Life Enrichment Model™. BACKBONE is anchored by the two *stabilizing* Enrichment Elements --- CAREER SUCCESS and LEGACY. They are characteristic of a mind-set cognizant of what it takes to achieve the level of financial achievement & self-actualization you desire in life.

BASE

BASE is the first of the three Enrichment Platforms. Base is the most fundamental component within the Life Enrichment Model ™. BASE is anchored by the two *foundational* Enrichment Elements --- SELF-AWARENESS and EDUCATION. These Elements, through Platform Archetypes, aid in focusing your thoughts on "Who am I" and "What can I learn" at the time you initially encounter a major life event. Having these thoughts *top-of-mind* should aid your efforts to capture a complete perspective of the situation, the surrounding circumstances and opportunities to shape a more positive outcome.

BRACE

BRACE is the second of the three Enrichment Platforms. BRACE is anchored by the two *action-oriented* elements --- DECISIONS and RELATIONSHIPS. They are characteristic of a mind-set cognizant of what it takes to strengthen the pursuit of your ultimate life goals and reinforcing prosperous alignments with others.

"CAREER SUCCESS"

CAREER SUCCESS is one of the two *stabilizing* Enrichment Elements which serve as anchors within the BACKBONE Enrichment Platform.

CONTINUUM OF LIFE

The Continuum of Life is the human life span viewed as a "continuous opportunity" for personal growth and enrichment. As you travel along the *continuum of life*, you acquire additional gifts, talents and wisdom as well as a deeper *awareness* and a broader *perspective* of yourself, your environment and others around you.

"DECISIONS"

DECISIONS is one of the two *action-oriented* Enrichment Elements which serve as anchors within the BRACE Enrichment Platform.

DELIBERATION MODE

The Deliberation Mode is the second mode of the Modal Exploration process. In the Deliberation Mode, you are enlightened by the development of a complete understanding of an enrichment opportunity which you have identified as a potential response to a circumstance at hand. This step of the process is completed by documenting *what will be required of you* and *others* in order to *seize* the opportunity.

DISCOVERY MODE

The Discovery Mode is the first mode of the Modal Exploration process. In the Discovery Mode the objective is to develop a concise summary and description of each circumstance surrounding the *event* or *situation* at hand. This activity is fueled by a thoughtful and thorough examination of all aspects of the situation.

"EDUCATION"

EDUCATION is one of the two *foundational* Enrichment Elements which serve as anchors within the BASE Enrichment Platform.

ENGAGEMENT MODE

The Engagement Mode is the fourth and final mode of the Modal Exploration process. In the Engagement Mode, you develop and execute the *action plan* required to seize the enrichment opportunity. While in this mode you will also perform the follow-up activity required to evaluate the actual outcome and its impact on your life's richness.

ENRICHMENT ELEMENTS

Enrichment Elements are core sub-structures that constitute the Enrichment Platform. As an aggregate, the Enrichment Elements influence what we think, how we think and how we perceive the circumstances we encounter.

ENRICHMENT PLATFORMS

Enrichment Platforms constitute the core foundation upon which the Life Enrichment Model™ is positioned. Within the model, the Enrichment Platforms figuratively represent the underlying social and economic structure inherent to the work ethic and dreams of the vast majority of the working populace. Each platform consists of two Enrichment Elements.

EXPLORATION MODES

The Explorations Modes are used to examine the enrichment opportunities which may be embedded within the circumstances that surface as a consequence of Life Events. The four Modes are characterized as the Discovery Mode, the Deliberation Mode, the Selection Mode and the Engagement Mode.

FRAMING

Framing is the act of capturing your state of mind at the time a circumstance is initially encountered.

GREATER GIFTS

Great Gifts are qualities which, as compared to other human gifts, more directly contribute to your ability to put yourself in a position to take the actions which will result in positive outcomes. The *greater gifts* are exemplified by the following traits: *Self-awareness*; *Imagination*, *Conscience* and *Independent Will*.

"LEGACY"

LEGACY is one of the two *stabilizing* Enrichment Elements which serve as anchors within the BACKBONE Enrichment Platform.

LIFE ENRICHMENT CONTINUUM™

The Life Enrichment Continuum™ is a paradigm that provides a systematic approach to characterizing the various *environmental, societal* and *human behavioral* factors that come into play when you encounter major circumstances in life.

LIFE ENRICHMENT MODEL™

The Life Enrichment Model™ embodies the concepts of the Life Enrichment Continuum™. The model is designed as a deductive and interactive tool to support your personal effort to enhance your ability to more effectively respond to major events and circumstances in your life.

LIFE CIRCUMSTANCES

Life Circumstances can take on many forms and can surface either physically, mentally or emotionally. In general, they are conditions or facts that determine, or must be considered in determining, a *course of action* that must be taken to *respond* to Life Events.

LIFE EVENTS

Life Events are noteworthy happenings that can occur at any time throughout your life span. Most events in life are fairly common. Most result in minor changes in your life and in your lifestyle. However, there are events such as the death of a spouse, a long-term loss of employment, a permanent disability, a chronic illness, an early retirement, a home foreclosure, personal bankruptcy and a teenage pregnancy that can cause significant turmoil and change in your life.

LIFE'S GIFTS

Life's Gifts are the natural talents and qualities you are given at birth i.e. mental, physical, emotional, intellectual and sensual abilities as well as those that you acquire via education, experience and maturation as you travel along the *Continuum of Life*.

MODAL EXPLORATION

Modal Exploration is a systematic process which uses a series of custom designed methodologies, queries and approaches to identify, prioritize and examine circumstances in order to seize embedded opportunities for shaping more positive outcomes.

OUTCOMES

An outcome is what follows after you respond or simply react to a circumstance. *Positive* outcomes tend to significantly enhance the level of richness in your life and have both near-term and long-term impacts. *Negative* outcomes seem to always be accompanied with setbacks and have the potential of impeding your growth and prosperity.

PLATFORM ARCHETYPES

Within the Life Enrichment Model™, Platform Archetypes are standards used to illustrate the essence of qualities set forth by each of the six Enrichment Elements.

"RELATIONSHIPS"

RELATIONSHIPS is one of the two *action-oriented* Enrichment Elements which serve as anchors within the BRACE Enrichment Platform.

RICHER LIFE

A RICHER LIFE is a life full of good decisions, financial security, great relationships, loving family memories and a feeling of completeness.

SELECTION MODE

The Selection Mode is the third mode of the Modal Exploration process. In the Selection Mode you must make a decision to either *pursue the opportunity* or to *respond to the circumstance* with another approach. A decision NOT to pursue the opportunity concludes this exploration.

"SELF-AWARENESS"

SELF-AWARENESS is one of the two *foundational* Enrichment Elements which serve as anchors within the BASE Enrichment Platform.

THEATER OF THOUGHT

Your *Theater of Thought* at the time you face an unexpected Life Event consist of what you *think* and how you *rationalize* the circumstances that have surfaced as a result of the event's occurrence. Both, your thoughts and your ability to rationalize can be influenced by what is presently dominating your "top-of-mind" and can significantly contribute to how you initially perceive the situation.

TWO-STEP OPPORTUNITY IDENTIFICATION METHODOLOGY

The TWO-STEP Opportunity Identification Methodology guides your thought process as you examine and prioritize opportunities and shape your responses to circumstances. The methodology is designed to identify the most favorable starting point or optimal Platform for entering into the opportunity examination process.

VECTORED CONSEQUENCE

A Vectored Consequence is the result of applying your perspective to *frame* or *view* a circumstance for the first time. The origin of such a consequence [one with magnitude and direction] takes the form of a set of captivating questions which attempts to illuminate the *difficulty of the challenge* at hand [magnitude] as well as the *course of action* that should be taken [direction] in response to the circumstance.

ABOUT THE AUTHORS

Ervin (Earl) Cobb
Charlotte D. Grant-Cobb, PhD

The Cobbs are widely recognized as two of the nation's *rising-stars* among Self-Improvement, Relationships and Inspiration authors, lecturers and speakers.

The collective seriousness and wit of their work has been described as perfect for "those seeking personal growth, change and life enrichment but not quite ready for Dr. Phil."

Their prior books include *Until I Change, Living a Richer Life: Getting the Most out of Life's Gifts and Circumstances, Pillow Talk Consciousness: Intimate Reflections on America's 100 Most Interesting Thoughts and Suspicions, Focused Leadership: What You Can Do Today to Become a More Effective Leader, Transition, Navigating the Life Enrichment Model™* and *God's Goodness and Our Mindfulness*. Their newest video lecture series is titled, *Get Ready to Reap All the Richness Your Life Has to Offer*.

They currently reside in Phoenix, Arizona.

SELECT BIBLIOGRAPHY

Andrews, F.M: 1974, "Social Indicators of Perceived Life Quality", Social Indicators Research 1, pp. 279–299.

Andrews, F.M. and R. Crandall: 1976, "The Validity of Measures of Self-reported Well-being", Social Indicators Research 3, pp. 1–19.

Argyle, M., M. Martin and L. Lu: 1955, "Testing for Stress and Happiness: The Role of Social and Cognitive Factors", in C.D. Spielberger and I.G. Sarason (eds.), Stress and Emotion, vol. 15 (Taylor and Francis, Washington, DC).

Blank, William: 2002, Soon You Will Understand, The Meaning of Life, Lincoln, NE, Writers Club Press.

Bowling, A.: 1994, "Social Networks and Social Support Among Older People and Implications for Emotional Well-being and Psychiatric Morbidity", International Review of Psychiatry 6, pp. 41–58

Bowling, A.: 1996b, "The Most Important Things in Life. Comparisons Between Older and Younger Population Age Groups by Gender. Results from a National Survey of the Public's Judgements", International Journal of Health Sciences 6, pp. 169–75.

Campbell, A., P.E. Converse and W.L. Rogers: 1976, The Quality of American Life: Perceptions, Evaluations, and Satisfaction. (Russell Sage; New York).

Clark, A.E., and A. J. Oswald: 1996, "Satisfaction and Comparison Income", Journal of Public Economics 61, pp. 359–381.

Costa, P.T. and R.R. McCrae: 1984, "Personality as a Lifelong Determinant of Well-Being", in C. Lalatesta and C. Izard (eds), Affective Processes in Adult Development and Aging (Sage, Beverly Hills, CA).

Craig, G. J. (1989). Human Development (5th ed.). Englewood Cliffs, NJ: Prentice Hall.

Edinger, E. F. (1974). Ego and Archetype: Individuation and the Religious Function of the Psyche. Baltimore: Penguin.

Hall, S. G. (1904). Adolescence. NY: Appleton.

Hunt, M. (1993). The Story of Psychology. New York: Anchor.

Johnson, R. A. (1991). Owning Your Own Shadow: Understanding the dark side of the psyche. New York: HarperSanFrancisco.

Jung, C. G. (1973). On the Nature of the Psyche. Hull, R. F. C. (Trans.). Bollingen Series XX. The Collected Works of C.G. Jung, 8. Princeton, NJ: Princeton University Press. First published in 1960.

Maslow, A.H. (1968). Toward a Psychology of Being (2nd ed.). New York: Van Nostrand Reinhold.

Maslow, A.H. (1971). The Farther Reaches of Human Nature. New York. Penguin

Reber, A. S. (1995). Dictionary of Psychology. 2nd Ed. London: Penguin.

Rebok, G. W. (1987). Life-Span Cognitive Development. New York: Holt, Rinehart and Winston.

Piaget, J. (1977). The Development of Thought: Equilibrium of Cognitive Structures. New York: Viking Press.

Washburn, M. (1994). Transpersonal Psychology in Psychoanalytic Perspective. Albany: State University of New York Press.

Wilber, K. (1993). The Spectrum of Consciousness. Wheaton, IL: Quest. First published in 1977.
Wilber, K. (1996). A Brief History of Everything. Boston: Shambhala.

Wundt, W. (1977). Lectures on Human and Animal Psychology. Bethesda, MD: University Publications. (First published in 1892)

Zimbardo, P. (1985) Psychology and Life (12th ed.). Boston, MA: Scott, Foresman and Co.

╪RICHER Press
An Imprint of Richer Life, LLC

RICHER Press is a full service, specialty Trade publisher whose sole goal is to *shape thoughts and change lives for the better.* All of the books, eBooks and digital media we publish, distribute and market embrace our commitment to help maximize opportunities for personal growth and professional achievement.

To learn more visit
www.richerlifellc.com.

www.ingramcontent.com/pod-product-compliance
Lightning Source LLC
Chambersburg PA
CBHW071307110426
42743CB00042B/1209